Donald K. Alper

BRIDGING
the LONGEST
BORDER

A History of
Canadian–American Studies
at Western Washington University

2021

Copyright © 2021 by Donald K. Alper

All rights reserved. This book or any portion thereof may not be reproduced or used in any manner whatsoever without the express written permission of the publisher except for the use of brief quotations in a book review.

Printed in the United States of America

First Printing, 2021

ISBN 978-0-578-75975-3
Library of Congress Control Number: 2020917421

Cover map: Steven Fick/Canadian Geographic

Author contact: donalper715@gmail.com
Bellingham, Washington

Editor contact: Catherine Wallace
www.wordworthymedia.com

To Bob Monahan ~ Friend. Mentor. Humanitarian.

Contents

Preface 1
1 The Setting 5
2 Beginnings 17
3 Getting it on the Map 31
4 A Flurry of Activity 45
5 Ebb and Flow 61
6 National Recognition 83
7 The Culture Turn 101
8 New Border Institute 135
9 A House Matters 155
10 A Border Runs Through It 173
Conclusion 199
Chapter Notes 205
Acknowledgments 214
About the Author 215

Preface

When traveling across the border from Blaine, Washington, into Surrey, British Columbia, it can be hard to notice that you have entered a foreign country. People look and talk the same, drive on the same side of the road, shop in stores with familiar names, and eat the same kind of food. The quite noticeable physical, human, and lifestyle similarities between the two countries—and the fact that the Canada–U.S. border is viewed internationally as a model of tranquility and cooperation—sends a strong signal that there is little reason for the American public to "understand" Canada and Canadians. What is there to understand with all this sameness? With incomparable historic amicability characterizing relations between the two countries, what can be learned that would be helpful? It is no wonder Americans pay so little attention to their northern neighbor.

But paying attention to Canada is important—even a matter of self-interest—because our family ties, natural resources, commerce, public health, security, and physical space are so intertwined, even more so in places like Bellingham, Washington, and cities near a border that stretches more than 4,000 miles from coast to coast. Canada is important to Americans because it is a major next-door country with its own national history, a dissimilar political system, and a different approach for achieving and nurturing social and cultural cohesion. For Americans, especially those charged with conducting political relations, a better understanding of Canada can help to avoid, or at least minimize, the inevitable squabbles that arise because of our shared geography, economic activity, and natural resources.

In the 1960s, a handful of faculty at Western Washington State College, encouraged by a few community leaders, set out to create a program for the study of Canada that would offer courses, encourage research, and provide expertise to business, government and other groups that wanted, and frankly needed, credible information pertaining to this important country. The result was the Canadian–American Studies Program, launched in 1971. When the program was founded, organized programs for the study of Canada were almost unknown in the United States. They existed at just a few universities, all located in the eastern part of the country. The program in Bellingham was the first of its kind in the western U.S. and today it stands out as a leader in the nation.

As a nontraditional subject of study, Canadian–American Studies at Western had to be invented from the ground up. The purpose of this book is to tell the story of the founding and growth of this distinctive academic program. The story of its development tracks with events that have shaped the wide sweep of Canada–U.S. relations, as well as more local events that have influenced cross-border interactions in the British Columbia–Washington international region. I wanted to tell this story to add an important chapter to the history of Western Washington University, and offer a lens through which the reader could view a sliver of the history of Northwest Washington and its ties to British Columbia. I also want to show how the work of this unusual program has become consequential in bridging the world's longest border.

From its beginnings, the program's aim has been to educate students and the broader public about Canada. Few Americans receive any formal education on Canada in their schooling. Even in primary and secondary schools nearest the Canada–U.S. border, it is rare to find courses that focus on Canadian subjects. In primary schools, the study of the Western Hemisphere is common, but most teachers choose to devote their attention to Mexico and

Preface

Latin America. At the secondary and college levels, the situation is much the same. Canada typically is viewed "not foreign enough" to be worthy of attention.

As this book reveals, the program's development reflects the foresight of a core group of faculty and supporters who believed Canada— so close and important to the U.S.—was worthy of study in its own right. They understood that American ties to Canada across the northern border have always been an essential factor in our nation's past and will likely be even more so in the future. More than an historical account, this book is also an argument for the importance of improving Americans' and Canadians' knowledge of one another to strengthen mutual respect and trust between our two peoples and their respective governments. Additionally, as the program evolved, faculty and community leaders realized that Canadian Studies research could yield practical knowledge useful for making better public policy.

This book is also part memoir. As one of the earliest members of the program, and its director for twenty-one years, it's been part of my own history as well. Now retired, and still living mere miles from the border, I remain convinced that ongoing education is needed to deepen time-honored bonds between our two countries.

Finally, this book is, at its heart, a story of two countries, but also an account of the pivotal role an early-1900s, two-story house played in influencing the way Canadians and Americans viewed each other and found common ground. It is a story of how this house— Canada House, located on the university campus in the topmost corner of the state—has become iconic of the affection and respect we in northwest Washington have for our northern neighbor.

1
The Setting

Geography and Historical Interdependence

To understand the significance of Canada to Western Washington University, it is important to begin with geography. Located in Bellingham just twenty-five miles south of the border, the university sits on Canada's doorstep. Although the border separates two nations, the ease of cross-border travel has made frequent movement both possible and desirable. Unlike most American cities, Bellingham is close enough to a major Canadian metropolis—Vancouver, British Columbia—to receive Canadian TV stations, make cross-border day visits easy, and allow people to live on one side of the border and work on the other. Local businesses depend on Canadian commerce, and Western Washington University has always attracted Canadian students, employed Canadian professors, and played in Canadian collegiate sports leagues.

In looking at a map of the physical region, Whatcom County, the county in which Bellingham is located, looks like it should be part of the greater Vancouver metro area known as the Lower Mainland. The cross-border region is what geographers call the Fraser Lowland shaped by the massive Fraser River that begins in the Canadian Rocky Mountains, flows southwest and spills into the Salish Sea about forty miles north of Bellingham. The lowland area, much of it shaped by the Fraser, is a relatively flat terrain bounded by the Chuckanut Mountains south of Bellingham, the Cascades

Range to the east, the Canadian Coast Range to the north, and the Salish Sea to the west. On a map, or from the air, the border appears as an artificial line cutting the lowland into two halves—there is no natural division. The American half is mostly rural with the largest city being Bellingham with fewer than 100,000 people. The greater Vancouver metropolitan area, with a population of about three million, is the dominant urban feature of the densely populated northern half of the region. Big city problems go with size and they spill into Washington state in the form of a high volume of southbound traffic, pressure on land use and recreation in Whatcom County, and heightened air and water pollution.

This unique border-spanning geography and size difference between the northern and southern halves of the cross-border region have made Canada a central part of the northwest Washington environment, economic setting, and mindset of its people. Even without focusing on Canada directly, academics and the general public must incorporate the Canadian presence into their outlook, whether in terms of urban planning, ecological issues, trade, retail activity or myriad border-related problems. The university is drawn to all manner of issues that affect the cross-border region, but also to unique opportunities presented by the close proximity of a major global city, several nearby Canadian universities, and a world-class natural environment.

In a broader sense, relations between the two countries in the Pacific West have been shaped by political and economic interdependencies as well as geography. British Columbia and adjacent western states share marine and freshwater basins and streams, forests, and airsheds. The sheer richness of the region's natural bounty has made for a continual and, at times, contentious struggle over management and exploitation of these resources on both sides of the border.

For example, salmon catches have always been a major area of concern for the two countries because fish spawning routes do not respect national boundaries. Salmon may mature in the Canadian Fraser River and after swimming out to sea, end up in the fish nets of American fishers on the U.S. side of the Strait of Juan

The Setting

de Fuca. Resolutions of disputes over salmon allocations have involved state and provincial governments, federal authorities, native groups, and commercial and recreational fishers in both countries.

Another vital resource that straddles the region is the vast forest lands covering a good deal of Washington and British Columbia. These forests and the products they yield have historically formed the backbone of the area's state and provincial economies. B.C. forest products, extensively exported into the U.S., compete with forestry operations in Washington and other states. Trade in forest products is complicated by different systems used to set prices in B.C. and Washington. There is also the matter of preserving wilderness areas, a cause that has particularly galvanized action in B.C. because the province remains one of the few places on the planet with old growth forests still intact. Environmentalists on both sides of the border—often working together—have long contested B.C. harvesting practices for spoiling some of these majestic forests that aid in regulating carbon in the atmosphere, promote biodiversity, and preserve sacred cultures of Indigenous peoples. Thus, Canada–U.S. trade in forest products, as well as efforts to protect wilderness areas, involve significant cross-border negotiation and collaboration. It should be mentioned that large forest companies such as MacMillan–Bloedel and Weyerhauser have always operated on both sides of the border. So too, environmental groups such as Conservation Northwest and the Sierra Club have membership organizations in both countries.

The coastal waters, encompassing what used to be called individually Puget Sound, Strait of Juan de Fuca, and Georgia Strait, and now collectively known as the Salish Sea, are divided by the Canada–U.S. border. The name Salish Sea recognizes that this marine area forms one large ecosystem that encompasses the surrounding densely populated urban areas of northwest Washington and southwest British Columbia. Harm to this ecosystem—whether by depletion of the orca whale pods or decline in shellfish—comes from urban and industrial sources, a growing problem requiring cross-border solutions. University scientists from Washington and British Columbia have cooperated to study the Salish Sea, and government officials worked for years to share information and policy ideas.

Perhaps more than other areas of cross-border interaction, the Salish Sea gives focus to the Indigenous peoples who inhabited the northwest coastal region for centuries. The name Salish Sea—in common use for only about a decade—emphasizes the historical unity of Coast Salish-speaking tribes and people who never recognized the "white man's border." They have their own sense of territoriality based on their traditional cultures and unique relationship to the land and sea.

Both geography and history have been strong unifying forces in the Pacific Northwest/Western Canada region of North America. For hundreds of years, the border was either nonexistent or so porous that few crossers paid much attention to it. Indeed, the Canada–U.S. boundary is a relatively new part of the landscape, having been imposed on the region by colonizing Europeans in the eighteenth and nineteenth centuries. Even after the political boundary was established along the 49th parallel by the 1846 Oregon Treaty, it was all but ignored by gold seekers, laborers, and immigrants who traversed the border seeking a better life. It wasn't until the twentieth century that the border came to clearly delineate two separate nations defined by distinctive national identities with dissimilar political and cultural institutions. Despite this, World War II and the era of free trade in the 1990s brought the idea of an emerging borderless frontier into play, indicating that the border was becoming once again concealed for the purpose of commerce, trade and continental defense. Since September 11, 2001, the border's greater rigidity for U.S. security purposes accentuated separateness and greater division between the two countries' outlooks and policies—a divide made only more evident by different Canadian and American responses to the COVID-19 pandemic in 2020. Yet, the enduring interdependencies derived from geography and history and historical social interactions are the essence of the Canada–U.S. relationship.

There is so much regional history in common, from centuries-old Indigenous connections, eighteenth and nineteenth century Spanish and British exploration along the Pacific Coast, northward movement of American explorers to the Fraser goldfields, disputes over the location of parts of the Canada–U.S. boundary, hydroelectricity ties on border-spanning rivers, the tribulations of transporting oil in the Salish Sea, to name only a few. Given this geography and history, and the problems as well as opportunities for cooperation it decreed, it was neither surprising nor unusual that Western Washington University would find it necessary and beneficial to develop an academic program focused on Canada–U.S. studies.

The Changing College Landscape

It was not inevitable that Western would develop a program on Canada. The college was founded in 1893 as the New Whatcom Normal School. Its mission was to prepare teachers, mostly women at this time, for the public schools in the State of Washington. In the early years, one to two years of teacher training was common. It wasn't until the 1930s that a four-year baccalaureate degree was authorized, setting the stage for the institution's eventual transformation into a four-year college. In 1937, the school changed its name to Western Washington College of Education. In 1947, the granting of bachelor of arts degrees was approved, which put in place the building blocks for a liberal arts college that could offer degrees outside of teacher education. Yet, even with new departments and programs, the school's emphasis on teacher training was all-encompassing until the 1960s.

Canadian connections were an integral part of the school's teacher education history. Western's proximity to the British Columbia Lower Mainland and the fact that teacher training programs were fewer in the province resulted in many Canadians choosing to get education degrees at the Bellingham college. When the college began offering programs for training administrators and other specialized education personnel in 1947, a new surge of Canadians planning to be school principals and guidance counselors took their degrees at Western. Over time, hundreds of Canadian teachers and administrators counted themselves among Western alumni, resulting in constant on-campus interaction between American and Canadian students and the development of a network of professional links across the border.

The changing nature of the college in the 1960s was important in setting the stage for the development of Canadian–American Studies. This period saw tremendous growth in student enrollment and new highly trained faculty. The state legislature changed the name of the institution to Western Washington State College in 1961 to reflect its expanded mission of serving students in the areas of liberal arts and sciences, in addition to teacher education. Several departments were created in the sciences, notably physics and chemistry in 1962. The social studies department was split into different disciplines—history, geography, economics/business/government, and sociology/anthropology. A master's degree in arts and sciences was authorized in 1963 and the Bureau for Faculty Research was created.

Many faculty hired at this time had earned Ph.D.s outside of the United States and thus brought a more international flare to the institution. Individuals with Canadian ties joined the faculty in increased numbers, adding courses and conducting research projects with international interest. Kenneth Innis, who emigrated from Jamaica to Canada, joined the English department in 1966 and developed the first courses on Canadian literature. Ingeborg Paulus, born in Germany and educated in Canada and the U.K., became a member of the sociology department in 1971. Paulus's courses on criminology were the first offerings on Canada's justice system in that department. Ray McInnis, a native of Saskatchewan, was hired in 1965 as head reference librarian. He studied at the University of British Columbia and received his master's in library science at the University of Washington. McInnis was instrumental in building a significant library reference collection on Western Canada and Pacific Northwest history. Manfred Vernon, born in Germany, immigrated to the U.S. during World War II and taught

The Setting

in Alabama before being appointed chair of Western's political science department in 1964. Vernon was a specialist in international law and served on the International Point Roberts Board of the Canada–United States International Joint Commission. Geographer James Scott was born in England, received degrees both in England and the U.S., and taught in Canada before arriving at Western in 1966. Robert Monahan, appointed in 1955, earned his doctorate at McGill University in Montreal and specialized in geography of North America, especially the Canadian and American Arctic. Barry Gough, a Canadian naval historian with degrees from the University of British Columbia and King's College, London, joined Western's history department in 1968. Bert Webber, a Canadian marine biologist with a Ph.D. from the University of British Columbia, came to Western in 1970 as part of the first-year faculty of Huxley College of the Environment. I myself joined the political science faculty in 1971, earning a Ph.D. from the University of British Columbia, and specializing in British Columbia politics and Canada–U.S. relations. Faculty with Canadian ties found it strange that so little was known about a country so close and important to the United States and especially to the Pacific Northwest region.

By the late 1960s, a group of inventive faculty, mostly from the history and geography departments, were advancing ideas for new institutes in regional studies: a Center for Pacific Northwest Studies, a Northwest Archives program, and proposals for a North Pacific Research Institute and an Institute for Canadian–American Studies. Those leading the efforts were Barry Gough, Keith Murray, William Bultmann and Larry DeLorme from the history department, James Scott and Robert Monahan from geography, and Ray McInnis from the Wilson Library. Pursuing expertise in cross-border regional studies was viewed by this group and others as a natural development for Western at this time as the college was expanding research, becoming more international, and gaining greater stature. Although an organized Canadian Studies program was still a few years off, the foundation was being laid.

It must be remembered that the late 1960s was a time of great ferment, not just in places like Berkeley and Seattle, but also in Bellingham. The Vietnam War spawned protests in Bellingham that received national attention, particularly when Western students blocked the I-5 freeway in May of 1970 to protest the expansion of the war into Cambodia. When Canadian protesters gathered at the border shouting epithets about President Nixon and then crossed into Blaine, Washington, where they broke windows at a local bank and tore down flags flying at the city hall and war memorial, they were joined by American protesters including many Western students. Western student activists found common cause with Canadians, particularly at Simon Fraser University in Burnaby, B.C., where students were embroiled in activities ranging from protesting American imperialism to mounting strikes against racism and sexism. Vancouver was a haven for American draft resisters, many of whom passed through Bellingham en route to Canada.

Activism on and off campus changed the culture of Western and contributed to changes in the way the college was structured. Students demanded a say in everything from faculty hiring decisions to curriculum changes. The college had become less hierarchical and students and faculty readily challenged established ways of doing things. New classes and programs appeared on peace studies, women's rights, ethnic diversity, anti-racism, and the environment. Faculty and administrators were divided on the shifts taking place in the college. Predictably, older faculty were less tolerant of student activism, believing that a college education was a privilege and students were at the institution to learn in traditional ways. Younger faculty, quickly swelling the ranks, tended to be more sympathetic to the students and many joined demonstrations, encouraged student strikes, and turned their classes into "teach-ins."

College presidents Harvey Bunke (1965–1967) and Charles J. "Jerry" Flora (1968–1975) had their hands full dealing with the upsurge of student radicalism. Bunke, a young and fairly progressive college president, was challenged by angry members of the Board of Trustees and the Bellingham community when psychologist

The Setting

and writer Timothy Leary, notably a 1960s guru of psychedelic drugs, was allowed to speak on campus in 1967. In an interview in 2000 for Western's centennial history project, Bunke said that the uproar by the trustees over Leary and their attempt to dictate college policy was what led him to resign the presidency. Flora became the new president and the beginning of his term was a calming influence on campus because he was willing to tolerate increasing student protests, did not crack down on the agitators, and even gave a degree of moral support to what was happening. When students took over the Placement Center to protest recruitment of people into the military or for jobs in companies that supported the Vietnam War, the president reacted by patiently talking with the protesters rather than confronting them with threats and legal edicts. As Flora later said, his chief concern was the safety of the demonstrators (the sit-in lasted about a week) because a group of angry students opposed to the demonstration was planning to attack the protesters who were occupying the building.[1] Flora's efforts, however, were not rewarded as he became an object of scorn by students who wanted greater change in the way the university was run. Later, when college funding was reduced by the state legislature resulting in cuts in the teaching staff, the faculty also turned on Flora by voting no confidence in his presidency.

This period was also a time when the campus and community were increasingly at odds. At a rancorous meeting at the Bellingham American Legion Hall in October 1970 intended to bring the community and students together, community leaders demanded that "Communist professors be fired" and insisted students "lacked discipline" and "had not gained enough wisdom to make decisions" about large political and social issues facing the country.[2] Bellingham was a small city run by local business leaders with typical conservative attitudes. Civic leaders, often a dominant voice on the college's Board of Trustees, were used to the idea that the college was run in an ordered, centralized way with a high level of regimentation and standardized courses. From the community's perspective, the college in Bellingham was a place for educating

13

future local leaders, serving regional employment needs, and was a source of civic pride. Suddenly, students were confronting traditional power structures and demanding that the college become an instrument of social and political reform.

With enrollment at about 10,000 students by the early 1970s, nearly double the number of less than a decade earlier, the college had evolved from the traditional state college model into a mix of semi-autonomous "cluster" colleges anchored by a large liberal arts and sciences program. The trend began with the creation of Fairhaven College and Huxley College of the Environment in the late 1960s. Both were attempts to create a small, experimental "college within a college" as an alternative to mass education and each enjoyed considerable support respectively from Presidents Bunke—who counted Fairhaven as one of his major achievements—and Flora who was a prime force behind the creation of Huxley College.

This was followed by the formation of the College of Ethnic Studies in 1969, which was a response to the concerns of minority students that the Western curriculum was devoid of racial and ethnic studies. Western had very few minority students in the mid-1960s although by 1969, with a concerted attempt by certain faculty—mostly within the education departments—to secure new federal funding geared to helping promising minority students, the numbers increased somewhat. President Flora had been a champion of Western's third cluster college and defended it—though most other high-ranking administrators did not. The College of Ethnic Studies was constantly under fire due to insufficient budgets, high staff turnover and enrollment problems made all the worse because of a "pervasive attitude against Ethnic Studies as a discipline," and not always concealed "academic bigotry."[3] Compared to the other newly formed colleges (Huxley and Fairhaven, and later Fine and Performing Arts and the College of Business and Economics), Ethnic Studies was given shabby offices in the old Edens Hall, further contributing to its marginalization on campus. When Flora's successor, Paul J. Olscamp became president, one of his first moves in response to an economic downturn heralding budget cuts, was to form the Program Study Committee in 1976 to review academic programs and recommend whether they should gain or lose resources, or even be terminated. The committee concluded, with the backing of Olscamp, that the College of Ethnic Studies should be dissolved. It lasted until fall 1978, at which time it was disbanded and the faculty were dispersed throughout various departments across the university.

Other new cluster colleges fared better. The College of Fine and Performing Arts was formed from several arts departments in 1975, and though larger and different in purpose from previous cluster colleges, the College of Business and Economics was formed in 1976, from a merger of the economics department and the various programs comprising business administration.

This time of change spurred greater experimentation in teaching, acceptance of smaller class sizes, a first interdisciplinary student–faculty designed major, and the growth of some multidisciplinary programs that stood outside traditional departments. Federal funding, mostly for science programs, accelerated in the late 1960s and 1970s, and faculty and departments were strongly encouraged to seek grants to augment instructional programs and pay for research projects.

In 1975, Olscamp, a Canadian born in Montreal, was appointed president of Western. He believed the time was right to elevate Western to university status by changing its name once again. The change to Western Washington University was officially authorized by the state legislature in 1977. Olscamp stated: "We are larger and broader in scope and curriculum and have a more extensive physical plant than 80 percent of the institutions in the country already calling themselves universities."[4] Except for offering doctoral programs, Western had indeed achieved university-level status by offering a comprehensive and diversified undergraduate curriculum, master's programs in most departments, a greatly expanded library, and significant research output from its faculty.

By the 1970s, interdepartmental minor and some major programs in areas including East Asian Studies and Women's Studies were either operating or in the planning stages. These programs were run by interdepartmental committees, and with defined curricula, but without faculty members assigned to the unit. Typically, a part-time director provided administrative leadership.

With a surge of faculty hiring between 1965 and 1970, and a demand for more decentralized and autonomous academic units, these and other new experimental programs were encouraged, if not always adequately supported. Among the programs would be a formalized Canadian–American Studies Program. Olscamp, who retained a strong affection for Canada and had taught in both Canada and the U.S., was bullish on Canadian Studies and believed Western should be competitive with the long-established Canadian Studies programs in the East such as those at Duke and Johns Hopkins universities. Without question, Western was becoming a rich environment for the development of a significant program focused on Canada.

2
Beginnings

An Idea is Born

The idea for a distinctive Canadian Studies program at Western appears to have first come from Dr. Robert Kaiser, a prominent Bellingham ophthalmologist. When he took Professor Robert Monahan's Geography of the Northlands class in the early 1960s, he hit upon the idea of helping the college create a Canadian Studies program. Kaiser, since coming to Bellingham in 1946 and even before when he worked in the Detroit-Windsor area, had been interested in Canada. His children went to school in British Columbia, he had many close friends in Canada and many of his employees and patients at his Bellingham eye clinic were Canadians or former Canadians. A worldly man who had traveled extensively, Kaiser was concerned by what he saw as estrangement developing between the United States and traditional allies He was especially troubled by increased anti-Americanism in Canada, which had grown with the start of the Vietnam War, and from pent-up frustration among many Canadians about America's enormous influence on Canada's economy and culture. He believed the two nations were drifting apart politically and thought a college program for Americans to learn about Canada would be helpful in improving cross-border relations.

In December 1965, Kaiser wrote Western President Harvey Bunke about his idea for an Institute for Canadian–American

Studies. He told the president that he had recently met with Monahan at his home, along with three other faculty members, to discuss what might be done. Kaiser explained that the group believed "there was a good chance that a project could be set up at the college, perhaps aided by federal funds, which could have a modest beginning but which could eventually develop into an Institute for Canadian–American Studies."[1]

Kaiser said those present at the meeting agreed to survey other colleges and universities to find out which have departments in the field, how they got started and how they are organized. Kaiser told Bunke that he thought the possibilities for a successful institute at the college in Bellingham were good because the city was located approximately halfway between the major cities of Seattle and Vancouver where the region's two flagship universities—the University of Washington and the University of British Columbia—were located, allowing easy access to the region's top research libraries and teaching staffs. Kaiser pointed out that the college's location on the Northwest Coast was a big advantage and could make for possible enlargement of the institute to include the study of other Pacific Rim nations. Kaiser asked Bunke to think about the idea and if he thought it worthy, his support would be welcomed and give impetus to the project. He concluded his letter with this observation: "The cost of one [military] bomber would pay for such an Institute for many years and think of the eventual benefit to our two countries that such a program could produce!"[2]

It is not known if Bunke responded directly to Kaiser's idea, or if the president had any interest in the idea of an Institute for Canadian–American Studies. Creating a new institute at Western would require funding from the college administration and commitment from faculty who were burdened with heavy teaching loads. Western was still a regional state college, hardly a research institution, and so the development of specialized institutes did not fit the college's mission. Bunke was focused on making Western a first-class liberal arts college. To that end, he set his sights on deepening the college's commitment to general education, completing the development of Fairhaven College and getting additional state support to hire new faculty for rapidly growing departments.

However, Bunke did seem open to doing something that would keep the Canadian institute idea alive. Kaiser, a few months after he wrote his letter to the president, sent a check for $100 to the library to buy books for Canadian Studies. Barney Goltz, director of Campus Planning, responded on behalf of President Bunke: "You may be sure that you have generated interest in the concept of a more formalized Institute of Canadian–American Studies which will get careful consideration by the academic planners in the months ahead."[3] Kaiser's donation would be used to establish a Canadian–American Studies account in the university business office, to be administered by Dr. Manfred Vernon, who was the political science department chair and a faculty member known for his expertise in international law and organizations. Goltz told Kaiser that the check would be formally accepted by the College Board of Trustees, suggesting that Bunke and the upper administration were at least familiar with the institute idea.

Kaiser, not one to wait for others to act, took his advocacy for Canadian Studies off campus to work his community connections and to contact members of Washington state's congressional delegation. In numerous letters to his Bellingham business friends, he explained that a Canadian Studies program deserved support not the least because it would be an asset to the community where merchants were more than happy to see Canadians spend and invest money. Convinced such an institute would yield important benefits for Canada–U.S. relations, he wrote members of Congress telling them of the importance of Canada to the community and state, of being troubled by the dangerous lack of knowledge Americans had of their neighbor, and asking for their support for the institute. In one case, when Congressman Lloyd Meeds' chief of staff wrote back with regrets, Kaiser wrote again, politely but firmly insisting on a reply from the congressman himself. He wrote Senators Warren G. Magnuson and Henry M. Jackson and when they did not respond to his satisfaction, he sent more letters. Eventually his letters piqued the interest of Senator Jackson who forwarded them to the Department of Health, Education and Welfare for consideration under the agency's International Education Program. The federal officials responded cordially but stated that existing law did not permit the U.S. government to fund the study of Canada through this agency. Kaiser did not succeed in getting the state's congressional delegation to help fund his Canadian Studies dream and, as it turned out, it took more than two decades before Canadian Studies at Western would be included as part of international area studies programs eligible for funding from the federal government.

In August 1966, President Bunke asked Herbert Taylor, dean of the research office, to prepare a report to the Board of Trustees on the concept of a Canadian–American Institute—what it would do, who would be involved and what funding would be needed. According to Taylor's report, a conference was planned for the spring of 1967 to discuss a proposed Canadian–American Institute with Dr. Vernon designated as the project director. "The Institute would conduct research and collect information on socio-economic and socio-political studies of the North Pacific Rim," the report stated. "It is proposed to, as the first step in developing such an institute, hold a conference on international law and the North Pacific fisheries problems—involving federal and state officials, local fisheries representatives, Canadian, Russian, Japanese and Korean representatives."[4] The report stipulated that the college's Bureau for Faculty Research would underwrite the conference while organizers would seek funding from federal agencies with jurisdiction over fisheries, interior and the like. Also mentioned in the report was an agreement entered into by the University of Calgary, the University of British Columbia and Western Washington State College for the purpose of researching and publishing a study of the Metis and Cree of northern Alberta and Saskatchewan, with the title "Investigation of a Northern Dilemma." The report stated funding for the project was provided by the University of Calgary ($3,800), the University of British Columbia ($1,000) and Western Washington State College ($2,700). Further, the document indicated that Oregon State University had agreed to cover 25 percent of the publication cost and distribute the book.

The fate of the proposed conference is unknown as a search of archival materials did not turn up any further mention of it. What is known is that the research collaboration among the Canadian universities and Western referred to in Taylor's report did lead to a large study (585 pages) titled "A Northern Dilemma: Reference Papers," edited by Arthur K. Davis, a prominent professor of sociology at the University of Alberta, and published by Western's Bureau for Faculty Research in 1967. The report—really a book—was a series of essays on the economic and social crises facing the Metis and Cree people following the influx of white settlers onto their traditional lands in western Canada.

This early instance of cross-border collaboration now looks like an isolated event as it is unrelated to a conference on North Pacific fisheries. Momentum for the proposed conference may have waned because of President Bunke's resignation as president in fall of 1967. Whatever happened, the concept of a Canadian–American institute had evolved at least to the point where upper level campus officials had taken some action, including supporting the publication of an important study on Indigenous communities in crisis in Northern Canada.

Kaiser's persistence helped to publicize the Canadian Studies cause on and off campus. Western's administrators had shown interest by promising backing for a North Pacific fisheries conference and supporting the publication of a significant book on the Metis and Cree people authored by faculty from Canada and Western Washington State College. It seemed just a matter of time before a Canadian program would begin to take shape. For that to happen, interested faculty would have to take the reins and drive the academic case for Canadian Studies.

'On the Doorstep of Immense Possibilities'

In 1968, Barry Gough, a Canadian who had studied history and education as a graduate student at Western and later earned his doctorate in naval and imperial history at the University of London, was appointed to Western's history department faculty to develop courses on Canadian history and Canadian–American relations, as well as teach other courses in British Empire history. At the time, Canadian history classes were offered by Professor Harley Hiller, who had done graduate work in Canadian and Latin American history at the University of Minnesota. Hiller's teaching assignment included two courses on Canada: a survey course titled simply Canada and a graduate seminar on Canadian history. Gough added to the existing Canadian offerings by developing a new course, Senior Seminar on Canadian–American Relations. He also was asked by Hiller to share teaching responsibilities for the Canada survey course.

Gough, shortly after his appointment to the Western faculty was confirmed and still in London finishing his doctoral studies, wrote to Hiller to ask if he would contact Robin W. Winks, Alvin Glueck Jr., and J.M.S. Careless, all prominent historians of Canada, to request information on Canadian Studies programs in Canada and the United States to give guidance to Western's effort. Gough and Hiller were also interested in starting a visiting lecturer series that would feature distinguished professors in the field of Canadian history. The two history professors thought to replicate a Latin America series, "Storm to Southward," organized by Hiller a few years earlier.

These communications set the stage for a forthcoming visit by Winks, who was invited to Bellingham in the spring of 1969 to speak on ethnic studies programs, as well as meet with historians to discuss Canadian Studies ideas. Winks, a distinguished Yale professor who had authored numerous books on Canada including *The Blacks in Canada*, met with several members of the history department at the home of department chair William Bultmann. As Gough recounted the event in a later interview, Winks said the college was "sitting on the doorstep of immense possibilities." The visitor from Yale was impressed by the prospect of creating a vibrant Canadian program in Bellingham because of Western's proximity to British Columbia universities and the depth of cross-border relations. Winks told the group that Canadian Studies was growing and diversifying in the eastern part of the country and the timing was ideal for something similar to happen in the Pacific Northwest. Winks' visit generated new momentum for Gough and his history department colleagues to move ahead with the planning for a Canadian Studies program

Following Winks' visit, Gough approached colleagues at Simon Fraser University (SFU), forty-five miles north in Burnaby, British Columbia, about a collaborative Canadian Studies program involving both universities. Winks had advised Gough and his fellow historians that Canadian Studies was more likely to succeed if it was structured as a cross-border partnership involving a Canadian and an American university with faculty and students participating from each country. Consideration of such a partnership was the subject of a preliminary meeting involving a group of six historians from Western (Bultmann, Murray, DeLorme, Hitchman, Hiller, and Gough) and four members of the history faculty from SFU, held at the Bellingham Yacht Club in November 1969. The model that was discussed at the meeting was the Canadian Studies Program in the Northeast, formed in 1967, that linked the University of New Brunswick in Fredericton, New Brunswick, with the University of Maine in Orono, Maine. This cross-border university partnership had a regional focus on New England, the Atlantic Provinces and Québec, and the two universities had created an exchange program for students and faculty to move between the two institutions. The idea of a similar cross-border regionally focused program with SFU appealed to the Western group, in large part because of the relatively short distance between Bellingham and Burnaby, the approximate comparability in size of the two institutions and the fact that SFU was fairly new and perceived to be more open to experimentation than the more staid University of British Columbia. Also discussed was an annual lecture on Canadian–American relations that would alternate between SFU and Western, a common research agenda focused on the cross-border region, and sharing professors in graduate seminars.

Following the meeting, a committee from Western's history faculty was formed to more closely examine two key issues that came up in the meeting with SFU: 1) cooperation between the two history departments on faculty and student exchanges, and 2) organization of Canadian–American Studies programs on a regional and international basis. The committee consulted with Western President Jerry Flora, the dean of the College of Arts and Sciences, and the college attorney—all of whom were "most enthusiastic about the prospects" of a two-universities partnership.[5]

However, in the end, nothing came of the proposed collaborative arrangement between the two institutions. Both campuses had interested parties, chiefly in the respective history departments. Starting some form of teaching exchanges among historians at SFU and Western seemed doable, but a more ambitious cross-border university partnership would require strong administrative and faculty action on both campuses. The time was not opportune to muster the needed support to move ahead. SFU was still embroiled in political battles that peaked in November 1968, marked by faculty strikes, students occupying administration buildings, and demonstrations challenging corporate influence over the university, and opposing the United States' war in Southeast Asia. It was also a time when SFU and other Canadian universities were developing their own Canadian Studies institutes. For the most part, Canadian Studies in Canada bore no resemblance to what was happening at Western. Many Canadian academics saw Canadian Studies in their home country as a needed corrective to the Americanization of Canada's economy, culture, and universities. Canadian Studies programs in Canada were inspired by concerns about the erosion of Canadian identity and the growing economic influence of the United States. It is doubtful that the formation of an inter-institutional Canadian Studies program connecting SFU and an American college could have been viable in this political environment.

By early 1970, an interdepartmental group of faculty members with shared interests in the Pacific Northwest and Western Canada had begun to gel, though there is no record of the group formalizing itself. These faculty are important because they would constitute the primary players in Canadian Studies and related regional studies programs going forward. From the history department were Barry Gough, William Bultmann, Harley Hiller, maritime historian James Hitchman, Pacific Northwest historians Keith Murray and Larry DeLorme, and from Fairhaven College American Indian history specialist Robert Keller. Additional members of the group were head librarian Ray MacInnis, geographers Jim Scott and Robert Monahan, and political scientists Gerard Rutan, Manfred Vernon and Oreste Kruhlack. Support for the cause also came from the administration, in particular from the dean of graduate studies Alan Ross. From archival documents, it is clear that Gough took the lead in the proposed SFU–Western university partnership dealings and he appears to have likewise played a leadership role in this group to push forward a Canadian Studies program initiative—without SFU. Another person who emerged as consequential in the effort was political scientist Gerard Rutan, who had a professional relationship with leaders of existing Canadian Studies programs in the eastern U.S. and the academic affairs officer at the Canadian Embassy in Washington, D.C. After coming to Western in 1969, Rutan, like many of his colleagues, saw growing interest and opportunity in pursuing teaching and research on the neighboring country situated just a few miles to the north.

In July 1970, Gough and Rutan placed an ad in Western's faculty newsletter inviting people to attend a meeting to discuss establishing a formal Canadian Studies Program. "Professors Gough and Rutan are interested in exploring faculty interest in a proposed program of Canadian Studies at Western," the announcement read.

> Persons interested in such a Canadian Studies Program are asked to contact either of them. It is planned that there will be a general meeting of such interested faculty early next fall quarter. As Co-coordinators of the proposed program, Professor Rutan and Gough would like to assess, 1) the identity of those interested in the possible program, and 2) the extent of interest among faculty in the building of an interdisciplinary program.[6]

Several faculty reaffirmed their interest in Canadian Studies, but no significant organization moves ensued as a result of the invitation sent by Gough and Rutan. Over the next several months, momentum for the establishment of a Canadian Studies program did not pick up. As Gough explained in an interview, it was not an easy time to get a new program up and running. Anti-war and racial justice activism was a pervasive influence on the campus and the attention of administrators and many of the more active faculty was on experimental programs that better fit the tenor of the times. Moreover, the Canadian Studies cause was not helped by the fact that many in the community (and likely a good number of faculty) held ambivalent feelings about Canada because it had become a haven for U.S. draft resisters and was experiencing its own political unrest in Québec.

Gough, for his part, favored creating a Canadian Studies minor as the first step in building a Canadian Studies program. He believed the courses required to form the core of the minor already existed and all that was needed was to bring those courses together under one area of study. But this was not enough, he maintained, if the program was to grow. Gough pointed to the need for certain resources and facilities, such as library holdings and meeting halls, to make Canadian Studies viable over the long term. Gough was optimistic about what could be accomplished and foresaw the day when Canadian Studies at the college could become one of the leading academic programs in the nation.

Much like Dr. Kaiser, Gough was troubled by the state of political relations between the U.S. and Canada. He thought a Canadian Studies program could be a valuable resource for improving awareness among the public as well as supplying research to help political leaders solve problems between the two countries. In his view, strong political ties between the Canadian western provinces and Washington (and other coastal states) would be even more important in the future as environmental issues shared by both countries become more acute. In an interview with the *Western Front* student newspaper in 1971, Gough seemed to anticipate the future when he expressed his worry that the new ARCO refinery being built north of Bellingham to receive oil tankers from Alaska would pose a serious pollution threat to coastal waters in the northern Puget Sound in Washington and Strait of Georgia in British Columbia. Gough observed that Americans and Canadians would have to work cooperatively on these issues to protect the shared marine waters. A Canadian Studies Program, in his view, would reduce misinformation that too often gets in the way of finding common ground on issues facing the cross-border region. Although misinformation existed in both countries, Gough believed it was far worse in the U.S. because Americans had little appreciation of Canadian identity and often failed to recognize that Canada is a distinct country.

In fall 1971, the college's administrative bodies gave authorization to the formation of a Canadian–American Studies Program at Western and the appointment of a director. No information could be found pertaining to discussions by administrators and faculty about program organization, leadership and curricular matters, which would have occurred in the lead-up to administrative approval of the program. What is known is that Gerard Rutan, chair of the political science department, was named director, with his appointment made official by the provost on January 17, 1972.

Rutan, a native of Montana, held a bachelor's and two master's degrees from the University of Montana and received his Ph.D. from the University of North Carolina. Prior to Coming to Western in 1969, Rutan was on the faculty at Seattle University. He specialized in comparative government with emphasis on Europe, the United Kingdom and Ireland. He had published a few articles on Canada–U.S. relations, and in 1971, he was accepted into the U.S. State Department's Scholar–Diplomat Program to research Canada–U.S. diplomacy. That same year, Rutan attended the founding meeting of the Association for Canadian Studies in the United States (as did Gough, Scott, and Monahan).

The exact circumstances that led to the appointment of Rutan as director are hazy. As discussed earlier in this chapter, much of the groundwork to conceptualize and build support for a Canadian program was done by Barry Gough. Tagged as a rising young scholar of Canadian history, Gough would seem to have been the most logical choice to be the first program director. However, Gough did not put himself forward. Perhaps he was not interested in taking on an administrative task as he was a relatively new faculty member in the take-off stage of a rapidly ascending career. When asked in a later interview why he did not put his hat in the ring, Gough observed that the Bellingham community was quite provincial, and thus the time may not have been right for a Canadian national to be named director of an international program at Western. Whether Gough was correct in his views about the Bellingham community, it is true that many American academics in Canadian Studies had insular attitudes about professors from Canada running these programs in the United States. An article in the first issue of the *American Review of Canadian Studies* (1971), the journal of the nascent Association for Canadian Studies in the United States, warned that Canadian Studies leadership in American universities was at risk of being usurped by Canadians who, like "missionaries," would use their influence to proselytize about making "Canada better understood—and respected—as a sovereign nation ... rather than building strong, systematic academic programs at American institutions."[7] From the standpoint of the community and college, Rutan was probably seen as a good fit for director. He had made himself available to local civic and business groups, chaired a department, was ambitious, and most likely had support from his political science colleagues and key officials in the college administration. He, like Gough, was quite active on campus in advocating for a Canadian Studies Program.

As it turned out, the appointment of Rutan as director was made when Gough was away in London teaching in Western's Study Abroad Program. Gough recalled what happened: "Upon my return, I discovered to my surprise that Dr. Gerard Rutan had been proclaimed head, or chair of the Canadian Studies Program. I was never given an explanation."[8] With archival information on the matter lacking and colleagues gone, I am not able to provide any clarity on the actual process that led to the selection of the first Canadian Studies director.

The new program was one of only a few in the United States that offered a multidisciplinary undergraduate course of study on

Canada. The curriculum was formed around a 30-credit minor that was applicable to the Bachelor of Arts and Bachelor of Arts in Education degrees. Course offerings were drawn from education, geography, history, political science, and speech, as well as recommended courses in sociology/anthropology and French. A review of the 1972–73 college catalog shows nine courses with a direct focus on Canada and five courses that included Canada as a comparative case. Of the nine courses focused solely on Canada, four were from geography, three from history, and two from political science. French language courses were recommended, although they did not deal with the particularities of Francophone language and culture in Canada. Fourteen faculty claimed to teach at least one course with Canadian subject matter.

The program was independent of any department and its organizational structure was through an interdepartmental committee in the College of Arts and Sciences with the director reporting to the dean. Faculty affiliation with the program was informal—normally just a matter of teaching or conducting research in the area. The program budget consisted of a small operations fund. No specific physical space was allocated. Rutan essentially ran the program from his desk in the political science department with no dedicated staff support. Library holdings were sparse and uneven in scope although with early support from the Canadian government, the Canadiana collection was gradually strengthened, with emphasis on British Columbia, Alberta and the Canadian Northern Territories.

Rutan wrote an article in the *American Review of Canadian Studies* in 1971 in which he expressed his thoughts on how students would benefit from the program. He explained the course of study would be of interest to students hoping to work in Canada or in organizations with business or other ties to Canada. In this regard, he said the minor would be a valuable supplement for students majoring in political science, history, geography, economics, speech, and journalism. Also contemplated but not yet realized was collaboration with Huxley College on courses and research dealing with pollution issues facing both countries. And, with a large number of Canadian students at Western, Rutan believed the program would appeal to them, especially those studying teacher education—many of whom already regularly took a variety of Canadian Studies courses.

Canadian Studies at Western was now a reality. Nearly a decade had passed from the time Robert Kaiser began promoting the need for an academic program at Western to inform Americans about Canada. A Canadian–American Studies Program was born, but it was totally reliant on course offerings in other departments, had no faculty of its own, no staff, and very little money. How the program would fare was, at best, uncertain. Nonetheless, the groundwork was laid, the initial hurdles were surmounted and the door was open for future undertakings.

3
Getting it on the Map

Program Development: The Early Years

What direction would the new program take and where would it get the resources needed to grow? Unlike a traditional academic department, there was no blueprint for a small, interdepartmental program focused on a country most Americans largely ignored. Goals would have to be determined, priorities set, and institutional support in terms of both funding and staffing would be needed.

The first Canadian–American Studies Academic Plan, 1974-75, listed the primary objectives of the program as: 1) raising awareness of all things Canadian; 2) encouraging and facilitating published research on Canada and Canada–U.S. relations; and 3) building a strong Canadian Studies Program at Western Washington State College. The academic plan also laid out specific future activities such as: establishing a regular symposium on Canada–U.S. relations; securing a dedicated Canadian–American Studies office; and creating and funding a core summer faculty to teach Canadian Studies courses and conduct research. Because Western had the only Canadian Studies program in the western United States, the program would be expected to provide academic resources, access to government documents, and information about Canada to K–12 schools, and other colleges and universities throughout the Pacific Northwest region.

As was the case with any academic program, the faculty and

curriculum were its core. At least a dozen faculty were teaching Canadian Studies and most were engaged in research on some aspect of Canada or Canada–U.S. relations. The 30-credit Canadian Studies minor was intended to be paired with a traditional major such as history, geography, political science, sociology, or English. The hope was that the minor might improve employment opportunities for graduates in areas of business, government, nonprofits or the arts, particularly where there was a Canadian tie. A Canadian Studies graduate program did not exist, although several departments offered graduate-level classes focused on Canada.

From the beginning, Canadian Studies faculty at Western recognized that if the program was to evolve into a major regional or national center, it would need to sponsor a wide range of non-classroom activities. Chief among them would be a funded research program for faculty and graduate students. In addition, conducting conferences and sponsoring lecture series dealing with issues in Canada–U.S. relations would have to be a priority. Program faculty and administrators were well aware that such activities would require external funding.

College funding for the program was quite limited. A small operating budget provided support for basic clerical activities and some travel money was provided for the director. All faculty who taught courses listed under Canadian Studies were appointed to their respective departments and their salaries, and most of the funding for any conference travel, was provided through their regular departmental budgets. Additional program support from the college was problematic, especially during the early 1970s when the college was undergoing budget cuts due to a weak state economy. Achieving the broader goals of the program would require finding money outside the usual university budget channels. One source of external money was Canadian government grants. Over time this would become a vital source.

Even before Western established a formal Canadian–American Studies Program, the Canadian federal government expressed interest in providing support for teaching and research on Canada at Western and at other colleges and universities in the United

States. In 1970, the Government of Canada issued a report titled "A Foreign Policy for Canadians," which stated that cultural relations with foreign countries were a vital element of Canadian foreign policy. In this document and in previous government reports dating back to the 1940s, Canadian governments were criticized for being far behind other countries such as the United Kingdom, France, and the United States in their efforts to provide knowledge about their own society for populations abroad.[1] What was needed, according to these reports, was a systematic effort to support educational activities in other countries to improve their citizens' knowledge of Canada.

In 1975, the Canadian government created the "Understanding Canada" program to provide grants and other forms of assistance to academics in several countries—including the United States—to teach and conduct research on Canada. The government's thinking was that supporting academic study of Canada in foreign universities would help produce people knowledgeable about Canada who, in turn, could inform their political leaders, the media and business types about Canadian values, culture, and institutions. The means for doing this varied, but they normally included Canadian government support for development of university courses and research on Canada in other nations, student and faculty exchanges, formal Canadian Studies programs abroad, and travel programs that would bring foreign students and faculty to Canada.

Western's Canadian–American Studies Program quickly took advantage of Canadian grant programs. In 1973, the Canadian Consulate General in Seattle notified Western that it was selected to receive approximately 200 books to assist in building a Canadiana collection in the college library. This appears to be the first Canadian government grant received by Western's program. In 1976, the library grant of $1,000 was received from Canada, beginning a series of annual library matching grants that continued until 2012.

Also in 1973, a grant from the Canadian Embassy paid for two 30-minute programs on Canada–U.S. relation featuring Western faculty that aired on Seattle's public television station KCTS. Canadian government funding paid the production costs, including speaker stipends and travel expenses. In 1977, the Canadian Consul in Seattle met with President Olscamp to discuss Canadian funding for a Canadian Studies high school curriculum project for Washington state schools. This project, which was funded in 1978 and eventually came to be known as Study Canada, began more than 40 years of producing Canadian Studies curriculum materials and workshops for K–12 educators, conducted by Western's Canadian–American Studies Program. Canadian government funding also supported several arts exhibitions and music programs, perhaps the most notable was bringing the Vancouver Symphony Orchestra to the Western campus. In 1976, Western was designated as an official depository for Canadian federal documents, an important step in building a diverse library collection of government documents and maps.

Looking beyond Canadian government grants, program faculty diligently sought foundation and other sources of funding to support program development. Indeed, early successes included a grant of $9,758 from the William A. Donner Foundation to fund a study of existing Canadian Studies programs for the purpose of making recommendations on the future design of Western's program. Also, in 1974, the Washington State Legislature provided $12,500 to fund the Symposium on Canadian–American Relations. A grant from the Washington State Endowment for the Humanities in 1976 supported a three-part conference series, led by political scientist Manfred Vernon and geographer James Scott, dealing with fisheries, oil transportation, and other environmental issues affecting the northern Puget Sound and Strait of Juan de Fuca. The series, "Man, Government and the Sea," was held in three locations—Bellingham, Port Angeles, and Tacoma—and marked the beginning of an enduring partnership between the Canadian–American Studies Program and the Bureau for Faculty Research, the well managed grants' office headed by Jane Clark and her second in command, Geri Walker. In 1978, when Scott and Robert Monahan received a National Science Foundation grant to offer a series of seminars for high school teachers on the "Implications of the Adoption of the 200-Mile Limit for the Nation in General and the Pacific Northwest in Particular," the dean of the College of Arts and Sciences, James Davis, wrote: "You academicians are cranking out grants, monographs, and articles, etc., so rapidly that it is difficult to keep abreast of all your activities. But we are grateful for your outstanding work, especially with the heavy teaching schedules you are carrying."[2]

A Landmark Symposium

Almost coincidental with the beginning of the Canadian–American Studies Program was a mounting concern about the deteriorating political relations between Washington state and British Columbia. In 1972, Dave Barrett, the leader of the left-of-center New Democratic Party (NDP), led his party to victory in the provincial election and became the new premier of British Columbia. The NDP in power marked a significant change in the ideological complexion of the B.C. government, which had been run by the conservative Social Credit Party, led by W.A.C. Bennett, since 1952. Barrett, a former social worker and flamboyant champion of the underdog who campaigned on the promise that his government would stand up to powerful corporations and protect B.C. interests, wasted little time in pursuing political actions—chiefly on environmental and energy issues—that put the province in direct disagreement with the United States and especially Washington state. What quickly became apparent to many academics, as well as worried politicians in both B.C. and Washington state, was the lack of any governmental mechanism to bring the provincial and state governments together to reduce bilateral tensions.

One hot-button issue was the Barrett government's determination to stop the raising of the Ross Dam, located in northwest Washington in the gorge of the Skagit River, 23 miles south of the Canada–U.S. border. Raising the dam would flood thousands of acres upstream from the border on the Canadian portion of the river. The dam is owned by Seattle City Light, a publicly owned utility company, and it supplied a good portion of Seattle's hydro-electric power needs. A contract between the utility and the B.C. government dating back to the 1940s allowed for the raising of the Ross Dam if future power needs required. By the early 1970s Seattle City Light claimed a higher dam was needed to generate more hydro power for a growing Seattle. The cost to B.C., however, would be flooding the upper Skagit Valley, resulting in the devastation of valued wilderness area on the Canadian side of the border. Barrett, taking the side of an emergent environmental movement that had strong support in both the province and state, vociferously opposed raising the dam. While the American defenders of Seattle City Light asserted that a "contract is a contract," Barrett claimed he had every right to break the contract because ecological considerations, not part of the negotiations in the 1940s when the dam deal was made, had become front and center in the current political and legal equations.

Many Canadian politicians and environmental groups sided with B.C. government's position. In Washington state, business interests and state and federal politicians opposed Barrett's action, not only because they believed Seattle's future power requirements would be jeopardized, but because British Columbia was seen as exercising bad faith by ignoring a longstanding legal agreement with a U.S. power company. Although the conflict persisted for some 12 years, it was eventually settled in 1984 by a Canada–U.S. accord— The Skagit River Treaty—which provided for the power needed by the Seattle utility to be derived from alternative Canadian energy sources. The dam was not raised, flooding of the B.C. valley upstream from the Ross Dam was avoided, but hard feelings lingered on both sides of the border. Interestingly, today, nearly 40 years after the Ross Dam issue was resolved, the upper Skagit watershed in B.C. has become a flashpoint for mining projects which, if built, pose a serious danger of polluting the Skagit River downstream from the Ross Dam on the Washington side of the border.

The Ross Dam controversy was not the only issue that jarred the traditionally calm political relations between the state and province. Like today, tanker traffic in the shared coastal waters was a potent political issue in the region. In the early 1970s, the U.S. Congress authorized the Trans-Alaska Pipeline System (TAPS) to carry crude from Alaska's North Slope, south to Valdez, Alaska, and from there to be transported on large oil tankers down through B.C. coastal waters to refineries at Cherry Point, Washington—a few miles north of Bellingham. Barrett, for environmental reasons and because he couldn't see any benefit for B.C. in the TAPS—only risk of devastating oil spills—announced in 1973 an alternative plan that would move the oil overland through the province and keep U.S.-bound tankers out of B.C. waters. The plan, known as "The Way Out," was to ship oil by rail from Alaska, south through B.C. (on B.C. trains with B.C. crews) to a location near the Canada–U.S. border, and then move it by pipeline to U.S. refineries. Barrett's plan rankled federal officials in both Ottawa and Washington, D.C., and threatened to disrupt energy development plans in Washington state. Though the plan was never implemented, Barrett showed his strong nationalistic streak and a willingness to upset normal Canada–U.S. diplomatic protocols to advance B.C. interests.

Of greater concern to Washington state was Barrett's determined and ultimately successful effort to get Canadian federal authorities in 1974 to hike the price and possibly curb the flow of B.C. natural gas sold to the United States. The Barrett government was intent on increasing the price of exported gas to bring it closer to world prices and end the practice, concocted by gas companies and their political allies, of British Columbians paying one-third more for B.C. gas than American customers in Washington state paid for the same commodity imported from the province. The gas price increase would be especially felt in Bellingham and other areas of the state with almost total dependence on B.C. for their gas. American newspapers pointed out that higher gas prices and expected cutbacks in supplies from British Columbia would place a heavy financial burden on Washington customers and lead to job losses in gas-dependent industries. The suddenness, and what seemed to Americans, brashness of this action and the magnitude of the price increase infuriated many Washingtonians, not the least of whom were Senators Henry M. Jackson and Warren Magnuson, who accused British Columbia of reneging on long-standing contracts and "seriously breaching the historical spirit of amicable cooperation between the two countries." The issue got heated to the point where one U.S. official declared "it was the United States vs. Chairman Dave."[3] A headline in the *The Columbian*, a newspaper in southwestern Washington, declared "The Blue-Eyed Arab Gas Plan Riles U.S." [4] The *Bellingham Herald*, concerned that cross-border relations were deteriorating rapidly, editorialized that "it is high time the leaders of British Columbia and Washington sat down and talked over the real goals and needs of the region" and "stop making hero speeches and talk common sense about common problems."[5]

Other troublesome issues were British Columbia's refusal to provide water and utilities necessary for the future development of Point Roberts, a small peninsula of Washington state land that extends below the 49th parallel and is only reachable from the United States by water or by crossing overland through British Columbia. Additionally, a long-standing conflict over salmon interceptions in B.C., Alaska, and Washington coastal waters upped tensions, as did Barrett's (unsuccessful) attempt to renegotiate the Columbia River Treaty.

Closer to Bellingham, Canadians were being blamed for purchasing about 60 percent of Whatcom County's available recreational land, crowding out American buyers, and inflating property values. This issue cut both ways as some Canadians pointed out that British Columbians had protested for years, without success, about Americans (many from Washington) buying up land in the B.C. Gulf Islands. "The piling up of cross-border issues and the apparent lack of any mechanism to address them revealed a complete lack of planning by the state and province in areas of common concerns," remarked a University of British Columbia professor. He referred to this inability of politicians on either side of the border to recognize the concerns of their counterparts as "49th Parallel Blindness."[6]

Even with the growing cross-border friction between the province and state, Premier Barrett had actually established a cordial relationship with Washington Governor Dan Evans, despite their very different political views. Barrett, when he held the position of Leader of the Opposition before becoming premier, took the unprecedented step of traveling to Olympia to meet with the governor. Later, in 1974, following a second visit by Premier Barrett to Olympia, the premier and governor decided the time was right to bring state and provincial legislators and executive officials together to discuss critical issues in bilateral relations.

In February 1974, Premier Barrett and Governor Evans issued a proclamation announcing a three-day Symposium on Canadian–American Relations to be held at Western Washington State College from September 19–21. Such a government-to-government meeting between a state and province was unusual, and in the case of British Columbia and Washington, it would be the first meeting of provincial and state legislators since 1925 when a similar, but much smaller gathering was held at the Empress Hotel in Victoria. Gerard Rutan, the director of Western's Canadian–American Studies Program, commented that "it is rather shocking that B.C. MLAs [members of the legislative assembly] and Washington state legislators had to wait 49 years to get together again."[7]

The symposium, organized by Western's Canadian–American Studies Program, was intended to improve communication and, many hoped, come up with mechanisms to reduce cross-border political tensions, making the meeting more than an academic undertaking. State and provincial legislators rarely met, mostly because issues affecting policy relations between the two countries were in the domain of the federal governments, not provinces and states.

For this reason, among others, the meeting in Bellingham was quite significant. The symposium format was designed to allow direct legislator-to-legislator dialog on matters of provincial and state interest without direct participation of federal officials. Legislators would be joined by academics, not only to discuss issues and propose solutions to problems, but also to engage in seminar-like discussions on the differences and similarities between the two political systems. The symposium would be, in the minds of its organizers, an important supplement to the mission of Canadian–American Studies at Western. In a newspaper article headlined "Historic Canadian–Washington Meeting Set," Symposium Director Rutan explained the significance of the meeting:

> It is becoming increasingly important to us that Americans understand Canadians and realize that Canada is a separate country with its own distinct outlook. ... Canada is our neighbor, our largest trading partner and our most strongly linked ally. ... Washingtonians are amazingly unaware of Canadian affairs. And like it or not, we are going to get more involved with our neighbor to the north.[8]

The Washington State Legislature, through a special appropriation to Western, supplied most of the funding for the event. Both Premier Barrett and Governor Evans agreed to attend. Washington contributed the most legislators, sending nineteen members from the Washington State House of Representatives and five from the Washington State Senate. British Columbia sent nine members from the B.C. Legislative Assembly. Numerous executive officials including some cabinet ministers from British Columbia and department secretaries from Washington also attended. The region's press was well represented with nearly fifty reporters from both sides of the border registered.

On the first day of the symposium, Canadian and American professors gave college-style lectures detailing the differences in government structures and procedures between the province and the state. An evening session, also run by academics, discussed the region in terms of its common geography and boundaries, natural resources and social and cultural similarities and differences.

On the second day, numerous panels were held, each with a keynote speaker and two legislators (one Canadian, one American) designated as respondents. The sessions focused on three areas of concern: 1) energy and environmental management issues; 2) land-use issues related to the B.C. Lower Mainland and Whatcom County; and 3) workforce and labor issues. Concluding the second day was a banquet and a keynote address by Congressman Lloyd Meeds of Washington state who represented the 2nd Congressional District in the northwest part of the state that bordered on Canada and included Bellingham. Meeds, after highlighting the top problems between the state and province—Ross Dam, Point Roberts, fisheries, energy pricing and transportation of crude from Alaska—spoke about the deterioration in relations between British Columbia and Washington state over the past ten years, blaming "ignorance, mistakes, demagoguery and misconceptions on both sides of the border." After receiving a standing ovation for pleading for "rational discussion" of cross-border problems, he made this telling observation on what he, and no doubt most people in the room, believed was at stake: "If Americans and Canadians cannot resolve their differences without provoking each other, then no one can."[9]

The final day of the symposium began with a session in which Dr. Peter Pearse, a prominent UBC economist and Dr. Charles J. Flora, president of Western, summarized the conference. Flora, making one of the more concrete proposals at the gathering, called for a follow-up symposium to exchange ideas on social problems where "both sides could learn from the experiments of the other."[10] Flora, probably wanting to avoid more cross-border meetings on hot-button disputes, suggested a parley on healthcare, as well as discussion about establishing liaison between Washington state and B.C. legislative committees. In Flora's mind, regular contacts between elected politicians who sat on state and provincial legislative committees would provide useful education about what the other side was thinking and also "early warning" of potential cross-border problems. This idea had considerable support from other participants, although most were Washingtonians.

The Canadian–American Symposium concluded with joint statements by Premier Barrett and Governor Evans followed by a news conference. Before a room full of reporters, the premier and governor reaffirmed their governments' commitments to cooperation but did not relent on any of their stances taken on issues, nor did they promise any concrete follow-up actions. Instead, Barrett used the occasion to tout his land-use policy—the Agricultural Land Reserve—a far-reaching zoning measure designed to protect much of the agricultural land in the province from future development. He also traced the history of labor in B.C. and made a passionate appeal for raising wages and strengthening worker's clout in the changing economy. Evans plugged a state land-use bill that was set to be considered in an upcoming legislative session and used much of his time to talk about an expected rise in Pacific Rim commerce and why the state needed to be better prepared to take advantage of it.

The lack of agreements on problems or any proposed mechanisms for improved cross-border communications disappointed many of the legislators who attended the symposium and was a point of criticism in several news reports. Looking back, it seems that legislators and the media were probably expecting too much. The conference succeeded in its goal of bringing legislators together to improve their understanding of how the other government functioned and how their counterparts on the other side of the border viewed common issues. Washingtonians and British Columbians learned that both the province and the state had their own interests that each side was bound to respect. If nothing else, participants learned that there were two sides to every issue and compromise, although necessary, would not be easy. Surely, Rutan's hope that Americans would better understand Canada as a separate country with its own distinct outlook was realized. Barney Goltz, a member of the Washington State House of Representatives from Bellingham, summed up what he thought was accomplished and the challenge ahead: "In some ways problems now look easier. I think it was a marvelous start for exchange. Communication alone, however, isn't going to get us over our problems."[11]

The symposium was lauded by organizers as an important educational event and possibly the beginning of a sequel of cross-border meetings and other cooperative actions. Some participants wanted to hold a follow-up meeting two years later in British Columbia that would feature a Canadian–American exhibition celebrating the history of close ties between B.C. and Washington state. Suggestions were made for more conferences to exchange ideas on oil spill control, alternative ports for tankers, healthcare, the energy trade, and land-use planning. Participants respectfully payed tribute to these recommendations but none were agreed to.

Much discussion at the conference centered on the need for a

Washington–B.C. joint legislative committee to help defuse contentious cross-border issues. In fact, the absence of a mechanism for regular communication among officials was a major factor in the symposium being held in the first place. Shortly after the meeting concluded, Washington State Senator August Mardesich announced that a special state legislative committee to handle Canadian–American issues would be recommended to the 1975 legislature.[12] Legislation was drawn up in both the state senate and house and final passage seemed all but assured. However, the B.C. government took no similar action which doomed the joint effort. The different political systems made direct legislature-to-legislature policy action awkward, if not implausible. Legislative commitees in the B.C. parliamentary system were mostly an arm of the premier and cabinet and had minimal influence over policy, whereas Washington state legislative committees had more independence and power. In B.C. the premier is the undisputed agenda setter for the provincial government. In Washington, the governor shares power with the senate and house, both of which have considerable influence over government policies.

Just as important in sinking the joint legislative committee idea was Premier Barrett himself, who was not interested in setting up a formal process that might be used to challenge his power. In his dealings with the U.S. on the price of natural gas exports and other environmental and energy issues, Barrett knew that he held a strong hand and that a mechanism like a joint legislative committee would only interfere with, or complicate, what he was trying to do.[13]

Although the state and province could not agree to develop formal means for government-to-government communications, there were nonetheless important symposium spinoffs of particular importance to Western. The most significant was the decision by Washington state legislators to eliminate out-of-state fees for British Columbia students attending Western (discussed in Chapter 5). At that time, British Columbia did not charge out-of-province fees for American students attending provincial universities. The Washington state action would provide the same deal for Canadian students that B.C. gave to American students.

Tuition reciprocity, as it was known, was intended to encourage greater numbers of students to attend colleges and universities in the other country. Another symposium spinoff was the designation of Western Washington State College by the state's Higher Education Coordinating Board as the primary campus in the state to offer Canadian Studies. Although the designation did not result in anything tangible (such as dedicated state funding for Canadian–American Studies), it did strengthen the identification of Canadian–American Studies in Washington state with the campus in Bellingham. In this regard, this new status helped solidify the Canadian program as a distinctive and emerging part of the growing liberal arts institution.

The 1974 Canadian–American Symposium was a formative event for the program's future development. It blazed a path for forthcoming Canada–U.S. conferences at the campus and established Western's role in the Pacific Northwest as the "go-to" place for public events on matters involving Canada. Western's strategic geographic position and growing expertise on Canada made the college a natural location for future seminars and meetings dealing with cross-border issues. The Canadian–American Symposium was an example of how the college could contribute to mutual understanding between the two countries and the improvement of B.C.–Washington government relations, in addition to offering a strong academic program on Canada for its students.

4
A Flurry of Activity

Leadership Changes

In 1975, Paul J. Olscamp was appointed president of the college, replacing Charles J. Flora. Olscamp, a Canadian by birth, viewed Western's developing Canadian–American Studies as one of the college's distinctive programs and wanted to see it prosper:

> I'm an advocate of a very strong and friendly relationship with the Canadian people. The U.S. and Canada are more closely intertwined than any two nations in the history of the world. As long as I am president of Western, I will try to cultivate a better relationship between the two nations. I feel very deeply about my native country.[1]

Olscamp worried that a "vast reservoir of ignorance of what goes on north of the border" was an impediment to a good working relationship between the two countries. In his view, a Canadian Studies program could help American students and the public better understand Canada and the mutual interests shared by both nations. He believed Canadian Studies had the potential to grow and become a signature program at Western and be competitive with the best programs on the East Coast—namely Johns Hopkins, Duke, Vermont, and Maine.

Olscamp worked closely with Canadian government officials at the consulate in Seattle and in Ottawa to help the program secure grants and attract visiting speakers. He was especially keen on the idea of eliminating out-of-state tuition for British Columbia students attending Western. As he saw it, a greater exchange of students would bring new perspectives benefitting not just the individual student but also the college, community, and state. He personally lobbied state legislators and his efforts bore fruit as the Washington State Legislature passed a measure to grant B.C. students in-state tuition that went into effect in 1979.

Within the leadership of Canadian–American Studies there was an unexpected development in store. On February 4, 1976, program director Gerard Rutan announced to the program faculty that he was resigning the directorship. Rutan's action came without warning and took the faculty and university administration by surprise. The notice of his resignation was transmitted to the program faculty in a memo announcing the next Canadian–American Studies meeting. The last agenda item on the memo read, "consideration of procedures for selection of new Program director."[2] Rutan then wrote:

> I include the last agenda item because I have come to the conclusion that it is time for a new director to take over the Program. I have been active as director since 1972, and have worked at building the Program since 1970. It is time for new ideas, new vistas, and new leadership. I plan to submit my formal letter of resignation as director to the President at the end of this academic year, and certainly before the beginning of the next. Thus, it is important that we meet to structure and to begin the process for selection of the new Program director.[3]

The following day, he wrote to President Olscamp restating his intention to resign, but also adding:

> I take this action because I am pretty well convinced that after all these years the Program needs someone with new ideas and vigor to continue building it. It is the good and the growth of the Program I am thinking of ... and that alone has brought me to suggest this action to the program faculty.[4]

A Flurry of Activity

Rutan's use of the phrase "to suggest this action to the program faculty" seemed to leave an opening so that he might retain the directorship should the president or program faculty so desire. Olscamp wrote to Rutan on February 17:

> Dear Jerry, I am distressed that you wish to give up the directorship of the Canadian–American Studies Program at the end of the present academic year. I can understand the very significant additional work load this has meant for you since 1972, but the fruits of your labors are so obvious and valuable that I cannot help wonder if the program will prosper "with new ideas and vigor" more than it did with your own ideas and vigor! Please do think about it carefully. I would be happy to talk to you about it if that was your desire.[5]

Geography professor Robert Monahan, who had worked with Rutan in starting the program, said in a letter to President Olscamp that Rutan's decision to step down from the directorship was probably related to his increased activities in Canadian Studies at the national level. Rutan had taken a leadership role in the recently established Association for Canadian Studies in the United States, based in Washington, D.C., He also had been appointed to a scholar diplomat program at the U.S. Department of State.

But Olscamp had doubts that Rutan's new national prominence was the reason, stating in a letter to Monahan:

> I will be personally surprised if Jerry's involvement in national and international affairs related to Canadian Studies provided a reason in his mind for relinquishing the guidance of the local program when that guidance had been so successful."[6]

What prompted Rutan's sudden decision to resign remains a mystery. I was aware that some faculty had concerns about his leadership style, which might have been a factor in his decision. Rutan was effective in getting things done, but some of his colleagues thought the program was too much of a one-man show. Despite that, he clearly had strong support from the president, a good portion of the faculty and Rutan was thought highly of by

Canadian government officials who provided grants and public support for the program.

It wasn't until May 3, almost three months after Rutan announced his intent to resign, that a Canadian–American Studies faculty meeting was scheduled for May 12 to begin the process of selecting a new director. The three month hiatus, seemingly long, provided time for him to reconsider his decision should he choose to do so. And there was no sense of urgency since his resignation would not be effective until the end of the academic year. As it turned out, Rutan stuck to his decision. No candidate for the position emerged during the long period between his resignation announcement and the May faculty meeting. Barry Gough had left Western in 1974 to take a position at Wilfred Laurier University in Ontario, so he was unavailable. As for other potential candidates, I was not aware of any, although at the time I had learned that retired, but still very active, Manfred Vernon could be available should no one else stand for the job.

Prior to the May 12 meeting, steps were taken to determine what constituted membership in the Canadian–American Studies Program for the purpose of voting. Thus far, Canadian–American Studies had no bylaws for determining which faculty were members of the program. Membership was simply a matter of having an interest in Canada—usually indicated by teaching in the area. In a memo to the faculty, Rutan said "he had been asked to prepare a list of active faculty members actually upon campus who are this academic year members of the Canadian–American Studies Program."[7]

The list included fourteen faculty who were judged by Rutan to be eligible for voting purposes. The list had notable omissions which did not sit well with some program members. Most outspoken was geography professor Robert Teshera who wrote to Rutan, with copies sent to other program faculty, saying: "I am deeply troubled by the decision to exclude several persons from *full* [emphasis from Teshera] participation in the Canadian–American Studies Program and am especially distressed at the exclusion of

A Flurry of Activity

Professor Manfred Vernon." He also mentioned the exclusion of librarian Ray McInnis from the list. Teshera, not one to mince words, further wrote that the action taken by Rutan—particularly with regard to Vernon—was "petty, cavalier, insulting to the individuals on a personal level and, on a general level, and it has strong overtones of academically unethical behavior."[8]

Although retired, Vernon held the title of emeritus professor, continued to teach part-time and retained an active interest in matters of international law related to Canada. In informal talks with me and other participating faculty regarding the future of the directorship, Vernon made it known that he could be available as a candidate for director should it come to that.

At the May 12 meeting, faculty members in attendance voted to recommend the appointment of Manfred Vernon as the new director. The notes from the meeting do not show whether the vote was unanimous or if anyone else was nominated. That the faculty turned to the retired political science professor is understandable. Vernon had worked closely with the geographers—especially with Jim Scott—in developing the Center for Pacific Northwest Studies and in organizing conferences dealing with cross-border issues. He started a TV interview show on KVOS, a Bellingham station which catered its programming to a Canadian audience in southwest British Columbia. Vernon's television shows dealt with foreign policy topics, many of which related to Canada-U.S. relations. A former chair of the political science department, he brought to the position important administrative experience." For these reasons and others, faculty colleagues could get behind Vernon's candidacy.

The vote of the faculty for director was a recommendation and, as was normal in selecting chairs of academic departments, required approval by the provost. No administrative action was taken on the vote to recommend Vernon for more than a month. In early July, President Olscamp, in an unusual personnel action, refused to accept the faculty vote for Vernon. Olscamp determined that "because of his emeritus status, Manfred Vernon is not an acceptable candidate for the position of the Director of the Canadian–

American Studies Program."⁹ Olscamp further justified his decision by telling the program faculty—including Vernon—that it would be inappropriate for someone who was not a regular member of the faculty to be in charge of a college budget. Olscamp then asked Dean James Davis, who concurred with Olscamp's decision not to appoint Vernon, to conduct a new election in the fall using whatever procedure he deemed appropriate. He also told Davis to speak with Rutan about continuing as acting director until the fall election was held.

Prior to the fall election meeting on September 29, Olscamp instructed Loren Webb, who had become the acting provost, to officially determine which faculty should be considered members of the Canadian–American Studies Program for the purpose of voting. This seemed to be a straightforward effort to clarify for the first-time those who constituted the Canadian–American Studies faculty. In all probability, a more important reason for involving Webb was to head off the problem raised earlier by Professor Teshera where the Canadian–American Studies Program director himself determined which faculty qualified as voting members for the purpose of recommending a new director. Webb came up with a convoluted scheme that created two categories of faculty: The first list included eight faculty who "directly teach in the area of Canadian–American Studies," and the second list included twelve "who are interested and teach courses that tangentially bear a relation to Canadian- American Studies." All members in the first category were giving voting rights, and all those in the second category "who wished to be considered a part of the program" were given the same status.[10] As it turned out, under Webb's almost comical voting formula, a total of 18 faculty were considered program members and thus eligible to vote for the new director.

At the meeting, Dean Davis served as chair and opened the meeting by asking for nominations for director. Before any were made, Professor Vernon asked that he be granted a point of personal privilege "to read a statement expressing his displeasure with Olscamp and Davis for refusing to accept him as director in accordance with the earlier vote." Following Vernon's statement, Davis said there was no precedent at Western or other institutions of higher education "for emeriti professors to serve as department chairs, program directors, or other regular administrative positions." Davis then asked for nominations and Professor Vernon was nominated again, but he requested that his name be withdrawn. Rutan was also nominated, but he declined the nomination. Professor Robert Monahan of the geography department, whom most of the members now favored, was likewise nominated. No other nominations were made. Of the twelve faculty present at the meeting, Monahan received eleven votes with one abstention. Following the vote, a discussion ensued about how President Olscamp treated the earlier Vernon vote. Several members wanted the meeting to go on record deploring the president's rejection of Vernon as director of the program. Feeling this action would be of no help in furthering the cause of Canadian–American Studies, the members decided to postpone consideration of the resolution. Following this, a motion to thank Rutan for his service was adopted unanimously.

In the wake of these bizarre events, Professor Monahan assumed the chair and, seeking to calm the waters, spoke highly of Rutan's accomplishments, noted the many significant scholarly contributions by the program faculty, and "expressed his firm belief that the Canadian–American Studies Program has a good future at Western."[11]

Monahan was officially appointed director by the provost on October 6, 1976, for a three-year term. He was a popular choice to take over the program for several reasons. He held a Ph.D. from McGill University in Montreal where he specialized in resource geography with an emphasis on the Arctic. He was a member of the Western geography department faculty since 1955 and had served for a considerable period of time as secretary/treasurer for the Association of Pacific Coast Geographers, which had a large Canadian membership. He was a leader in the Canadian Association of Geographers and was also in the group that founded ACSUS in 1971.

Additionally, he was an active participant in Western's early efforts to develop cross-border regional studies, and was involved with the group of faculty who established the Canadian–American Studies Program. He was known as a team player, an important quality for any director faced with the difficult task of enlisting and sustaining faculty commitment to a still relatively new interdepartmental program.

Monahan began his directorship with a flurry of activity. One of his first actions was to survey faculty to identify everyone who was involved in teaching and research on Canadian topics. The result was a 1976–77 Canadian–American Studies faculty roster that listed twenty-four participating faculty—a substantial increase from the previous count of fourteen listed in the 1972–73 catalog. The majority of those faculty came from geography (6), history (5), political science (4), and anthropology (2); English, sociology, economics, French, speech, education and library each had one. Subcommittees were formed in the key areas of curriculum development, grants and speakers.

With Monahan's encouragement, program faculty submitted several grant proposals to the newly created Canadian–American Studies Research Grants Program. The funded projects indicate the range of faculty and graduate student interests in this early period of the program. For example, William Bultmann of the history department wrote a history of the Canadian Gulf Islands; Kenneth Inniss of the English department researched the history of Victoria's first Black settlers using archival records of the first Colonial Governor of British Columbia; geography professor Debnath Mookherjee examined Canadian patronage of Bellingham businesses; Peter Haye of the College of Performing Arts studied the formation of cultural exchanges—artists, musicians and exhibits— between B.C. and Washington and how exchanges could be expanded; Lorena Welty, graduate student in the history department investigated factors contributing to peaceful resolution of boundary disputes along the Canada–U.S. border; Dan Boxberger, anthropology graduate student and later a member of Western's faculty researched Indian and First Nation treaties utilizing the provincial archives of British Columbia; my own project examined attitudes of members of the U.S. Congress toward Canada. The university provided $28,000 for the research program, an unusual move at Western where research budgets were almost nonexistent in the social sciences departments. The research funding was an important statement of early university support and, it seemed, a vote of confidence in the new director.

Teaching a full course load and still encumbered by geography department committee duties, Monahan knew he needed help. He believed the program needed an associate director to assist with expanded program activities, particularly K–12 outreach, conference organization and assistance with writing grants. Moreover, he was aware of the danger of allowing the program to be overly centered on, and identified with, one person, a problem that arose during Rutan's directorship. Also important was the matter of mentoring someone who could succeed to the directorship when Monahan was ready to retire or step down.

Because Monahan and I had worked together on Canadian Studies projects and I was a political scientist who had lived and studied in Canada, he thought I would be a good choice for associate director. At the time there was no such position and we both knew the one being contemplated would be in effect voluntary with no release time or extra pay. I had become more involved in the program in 1975 when I participated in a series of forums on the impacts of increased oil tanker traffic in the Salish Sea, organized by Manfred Vernon and geographer James Scott. Although I was not tenured, the prospect of becoming more involved in the Canadian–American Studies Program appealed to me. I worked under two of Canada's top political scientists, Alan Cairns and Walter Young, during my doctoral studies at the University of British Columbia, and spent six months in Ottawa working for a member of the Canadian House of Commons. With this experience and my growing interest in the Canadian–American Studies Program, I thought being part of this venture would be fulfilling and a lot of fun. Besides, Monahan and I had become good friends and that made it easy to accept the associate director position, which he offered to me soon after becoming director.

From Program to Center

With leadership in place, other major changes were on the agenda for growing the program. At the first Canadian–American Studies Program meeting following Monahan's appointment, a discussion ensued on changing the name to "Center." Faculty knowledgeable about federal grants reminded the group that funding through the National Defense Education Act Title VI program was "going to Canadian Studies 'Centers' or 'Institutes.'" The general opinion at the meeting was that a change in name from program to center "would increase visibility and enhance our ability to achieve grants."[12] By this time—the late 1970s—Canadian Studies organizations at Duke University, the University of Vermont, the University of Maine, and SUNY–Plattsburgh all had been awarded federal Title VI funding. Each of these institutions used the word "Center" in the names of their Canadian Studies programs.

The proposed name change was part of a broader effort to take the program to the next level. In 1977, a long-term academic plan set out an ambitious agenda for a future Center. Following the statement of core goals of expanding curricular offerings, research and K–12 educational outreach, the plan spoke to the importance of studying Canada as a nation in its own right:

> In studying Canada and things Canadian, the understanding of our own country and culture is enhanced and creativity, understanding, and positive action or the mutual good of the two [countries] is encouraged and stimulated. Informed judgment, tolerance, an increased aesthetic sensitivity, and an understanding of the historical continuity flow from a study of Canadian topics and Canadian and American concerns.[13]

In the past, the program had emphasized the Pacific Northwest–British Columbia region. The new planning document stated it was necessary to have a national focus to fully understand both the B.C.–

Washington international region and the Canadian nation as a whole:

> The present and future needs of Washington State will require more knowledge and better understanding of British Columbia because of the interrelations of our environment, our resources, our economies, and our peoples. While the focus is on British Columbia, this cannot be fully understood, nor can things be accomplished without some understanding of the rest of Canada and the involvement of the national government in international affairs. Therefore our need to study and understand Canada and Canadians is boundless.[14]

This broader conception of the program recognized the value and importance of studying Canada and the people, places, and values that form the nation. It also opened the door to more comparative study of Canada and the United States and other nations. Scholars and students not centrally involved in Canadian Studies would find value in comparing the different ways each country dealt with social, economic, environmental and other issues.

The name change was approved to take effect in fall 1978. The name would change from "Canadian–American Studies Program" to the "Center for Canadian and Canadian–American Studies." The new name would better represent the range of academic and outreach activities undertaken under the Canadian–American Studies umbrella at Western. And, by being recognized as a Center, opportunities for securing federal grants were improved.

Other needs outlined in the planning document and eventually met were secretarial assistance for the director, increased funds for research, and the establishment of faculty and student exchanges. A new Canadian Studies 50-credit major was in the developmental stages and scheduled to take effect by fall. Also in the works was a new introductory interdisciplinary "core course" that would cover history, geography, government and societal aspects of Canada. Additionally, the Center would continue to engage in promotion of the teaching of Canada in the public schools in Washington, and serve as a regional resource and data center to store and make available Canadian information for use by academic, governmental, commercial and other groups. The pieces were in place for the Center to move forward. One important item mentioned in the plan that still needed action was finding suitable space for the growing program.

A Home of its Own

Since its inception in 1971, Canadian–American Studies had no physical space of its own. Directors Rutan and Monahan had operated the program from their home departments—political science and geography respectively. Secretarial assistance was minimal and generally shared with other administrative units. Without separate space, Canadian Studies activities were seen as an appendage of whichever department the director belonged. Acquiring some kind of separate facility was now considered vital to the success of the new Center. The Canadian–American Studies plan addressed the space issue directly, stating that the long-term vitality of the new Center required that it be housed in a separate structure to "provide a physical identity for the program and divest the direction of the program from association with a single department."[15]

Monahan wrote to President Olscamp on April 12, 1977, explaining the need for space and particularly an "independent building to provide offices for visiting scholars, hold seminars, and provide research space," among other functions. Monahan pointed out that having the Center in its own building would give Canadian–American Studies a distinctiveness on campus and provide a neutral administrative home for the program because it would be separate from any particular academic department. He also said he wanted the structure to "function as a 'Canada House' for the 200-plus Canadians currently in residence on the campus."[16]

Monahan, ever the geographer, checked out every space possibility on campus, including several old houses that had become part of Western as the campus expanded its footprint over the years. At one point, he suggested moving into an underutilized dormitory building at Fairhaven College on the southern edge of campus, but the idea was abandoned when college administrators estimated that at least $75,000 would need to be expended for renovation, leasing and maintenance costs.

Another possibility was the Campus Christian Ministry building, a property formerly owned by several Protestant churches, that had been acquired by Western as part of its long-range expansion plan. This Victorian style house located on Garden Street down the hill from the student union building would be available in 1978 when the print services and purchasing offices, then occupying the building, were slated to move out. College administrators, however, had other plans for this facility. There was also the Stearns House, a former boarding house located on the hilltop south of College Hall. After its student rooming house days were over, the house was used for office space by the education department and after that, it served as a studio for the art department. By 1977, the Stearns House was in disrepair and without an extensive and costly renovation it would be unsuitable for the desired office and seminar space Monahan envisioned. In the 1990s, the once attractive Stearns house, full of asbestos, and deemed by campus planners as not worth saving, was torn down to make way for a parking lot.

Eventually, Monahan placed his sights on the partially used former home of Western presidents, located on High Street on the westside of campus next to the Performing Arts Center. At the time, the building—known as the President's House—was being used for storage and rehearsal practices by the music department. The house was centrally located, in fairly good condition, close to parking, and with about 3,500 square feet had ample space for the program to grow. With President Olscamp's blessing, the deal was done and Canadian–American Studies moved into the President's House in 1977.

The handsome two-story, four-bedroom Craftsman with its quaint architectural details was built by businessman Henry Schupp as his private home in 1909. At that time, the house sat just outside the perimeter of the then small teaching college, located on a high bluff above Garden Street overlooking Bellingham Bay and the

Coast Range Mountains in Canada in the distance. On its completion in 1909, stories in the *Bellingham Herald* referred to it as "one of Bellingham's finest residences"; ... a "handsome structure"... with "massive Chuckanut stone walls for basement and veranda support."

In 1959, the house was bought by Western for $20,000 (which included 2 acres) to be used as the residence for college presidents. Three presidents lived in the house from 1959 to 1969. The last president to live there, Dr. Charles J. Flora, found the house too small for presidential receptions and dinners, and moved to a new residence outside of Bellingham. College lore has it that Flora was also encouraged to move away from the campus because of increased anti-war protests at Western in the late 1960s. The home of a college president situated on campus was a prime target for campus demonstrations.

Hassles over space are endemic to all universities and Western is no different. The music department was not happy about losing the use of the President's House. Once the house was given to Canadian–American Studies, other programs grumbled, particularly the Center for East Asian Studies, who wanted the same deal Canadian–American Studies got. And, the Faculty Club, a soon to be formed social organization at Western would have its eye on the charming building with its fine view of Bellingham Bay, stately parlor with a fireplace, and aged oak floors. As it turned out, this house, used as a provisional storage facility for the past eight years, had become the object of considerable controversy, and desire, by 1977.

But the Center for Canadian–American Studies prevailed. Canada House was formally dedicated on February 9, 1979, in a ceremony officiated by Canadian Consul General in Seattle, J.C. Gordon Brown. Before a crowd of more than 225 people, including Congressman Al Swift and several Bellingham city and county officials, Brown presented to President Olscamp a gift from the Canadian government of three framed prints by Canadian First Nations artists. Featured speaker Dr. J. Lewis Robinson, a prominent University of British Columbia geographer and a firm supporter of strengthening education of both American and Canadian citizens about the importance of Canada–U.S. relations, told the audience, "Canadians and Americans are guilty of having stereotypes of one another.... This organization will help to remove some of those stereotypes."[17]

As Monahan had predicted, Canada House gave Canadian Studies at Western a stronger identity on campus and in the region. It quickly became a hub for various seminars and receptions headlined by Canadian ambassadors and other government officials. Its proximity to the border and an easy drive along Interstate 5 between Vancouver, B.C. and Seattle, made for a convenient gathering place. The handsome early-20th century building was now hosting formal and casual meetings, social receptions, and small-scale seminars in the erstwhile living and dining rooms downstairs, while administrative offices occupied the upstairs bedrooms. The once small program, which had grown into a viable Center had gained a degree of autonomy and visibility essential for its long-term success. Having secured its physical place, Canadian–American Studies would nonetheless always have to defend the fort against groups wanting what Western's Canadian program now had: a home of its own.

5
Ebb and Flow

Program Development: Late 1970s and 1980s

On January 22, 1980, the Canadian Ambassador to the United States, Peter Towe, gave a speech at Western in which he observed that the university had developed "one of the finest multi-disciplinary centres of Canadian–American studies in North America."[1] By the time Towe gave his address, Canadian–American Studies had achieved a critical mass. In place were a major and minor with increased numbers of students, a wide-ranging curriculum with 23 courses from eight departments, a research budget, a curriculum development program for K–12 teachers, a growing library collection of Canadian materials, and a dedicated building on campus called Canada House. Indeed, the Center for Canadian and Canadian–American Studies had become a distinctive part of Western Washington University and Canadian and U.S. governments regularly interacted with the program and viewed it as an important resource for informing citizens about the relationship between the two countries.

The Center's future development, however, required far more resources than the university was willing to provide. Without question, program expansion would depend on securing funding from outside the university. The outlook from private funders was not bright, as companies and foundations tended to focus on large research universities with strong track records in fundraising.

Moreover, most companies were interested in funding projects they believed to be of direct benefit to their corporate mission. When we approached the Weyerhaeuser Corporation, one of the world's largest forest products firms—with offices on both sides of the border—for support in 1979, we were told in no uncertain terms that although educating Americans about Canada was worthy, it was not an area that fit the company's funding guidelines. The mission statements of companies such as Weyerhaeuser and other American corporations with business dealings in Canada did not include improving Americans' knowledge of Canada. During this time, some grants were received from companies that did business in the Bellingham area, but the amounts were small and usually earmarked for bringing visiting speakers to campus who were of interest to the funder.

With private funding problematic, government support was the Center's best hope. Since the mid-1970s, the Center was receiving financial support from the Canadian government's "Understanding Canada" program. This funding was used to develop courses, conduct research, bring in speakers, procure library resources, and fund special projects.

In 1978, the Center received $15,000 from the Canadian government, its largest grant to that time, to support a two-year K–12 curriculum development project—later named Study Canada. The project's aim was to educate American K–12 teachers about Canada so they would be prepared to teach Canadian subject matter in their schools. "It is especially important for the generation now in school to have an adequate information base to interact effectively with Canada," wrote program director Robert Monahan.

> The increasing importance of Canadian [natural] resources, the moves toward an economic partnership, the intertwining resource management, the [natural] resource movement corridors across Canada, the military agreements and the long friendship of the two nations spur the need for knowledge among Americans.[2]

Subject matter on Canada was a rarity in American elementary and high school classrooms. In most states, about the only place Canada turned up in schools' curricula was in the 5th or 6th grades as part of the study of the Western Hemisphere, where Canada was usually joined with Mexico and South American countries. A common practice for publishers of elementary textbooks was to place the Canada section in the back of the book. As we learned when examining how these texts were used, many teachers said they ran out of time in the semester before getting to Canada. With help from Donald Wilson, a former public school teacher and a professor of curriculum studies at the University of British Columbia, and Marion Salinger, a long time program manager for the Canadian Studies Center at Duke University, we sought out publishers in California and Texas and eventually had some success in convincing them to strengthen and even relocate the Canada sections in their texts.

The 1978 curriculum development grant provided funds for Canadian–American Studies faculty to develop educational materials and offer Canadian Studies summer institutes for K–12 teachers. In the summer of 1978, thirty K–12 teachers attended the first institute organized by the Center. Faculty from Western and the University of British Columbia taught the workshop in close collaboration with the participating teachers who drew on their own practical experience to advise us on how Canadian subjects could be fit into courses that varied greatly across school districts.

Among those attending that first institute was a contingent of four outstanding high school teachers from Vancouver, Washington, located in southwest Washington near the Oregon border. The Vancouver group—two of whom cycled the 250-mile trip to Bellingham that summer—came up with forward-looking curriculum ideas that formed the core of the first Study Canada published materials. "Study Canada—Overview," the first curriculum guide, covered the usual subjects of history, geography and government, but it also focused on Canada's Francophone societies and how Canada viewed its role in the world and its relations with the United States. The comparative method was used to show how Canadian society was both different and similar from the United States. An important takeaway we received from the teachers was: Make Canadian Studies materials easily adaptable to *existing* courses, rather than expect teachers to create *new* courses on Canada—the latter an almost impossible task considering all the subjects American teachers are required to teach. As we learned, success in bringing Canada subject matter into America's classrooms would require strategies designed not only for teachers, but also aimed at school curriculum specialists, state education supervisors and textbook publishers.

Following the second institute held in 1979, three curriculum guides were produced and disseminated to hundreds, and later, after being revised and updated, to thousands of American teachers. Thus began the Study Canada Summer Institutes annually funded in part by the Government of Canada until 2011, and then continued in different formats with other funding up to the present day. Study Canada became a signature program of the Center and it gained a reputation as one of the top Canadian Studies teacher education programs in the country.

Also in 1979, the Canadian government selected Western as one of three American universities to receive Canadian government grants annually to fund library acquisitions, with an initial grant of $2,500 to be used for book purchases. With interest building in the program, the library designated a staff member to be in charge of Canadian–American Studies acquisitions, much like what was common practice for the various academic departments. About this time the library received a collection of Canadian maps and became a depository for B.C. and federal government documents. Later in 1987 faculty librarian Rob Lopresti, whose scholarly publications, novels and mystery stories won him many awards, was named research and instruction librarian to the Center.

During this period the Center in collaboration with other programs made plans to build a cross-border research and data center to be located at Western. The data center, an idea first discussed at the 1974 Canadian–American Symposium, would store and make available Canadian-related information for use by academic, governmental, commercial and other groups. Envisaged was a central clearing house to contain statistical and nonstatistical information on Canadian topics of regional and international significance. The idea was attractive to academics and political leaders who believed more and better information was needed to research and teach about vexing cross-border trade and environmental issues, particularly in the B.C.-Washington region.

Relevance to the West Coast would be the major criterion governing decisions about what information to include in the data center. The clearinghouse would be under the control of the director of the Center, in cooperation with the head of the computer technology program and the university library. A chief editor would have responsibility for the processing, storing and retrieval of information, to be assisted by programmers and keyboard personnel, graduate assistants and secretarial staff.

A faculty committee, led by geographer James Scott and the dean of research, Sam Kelly, was charged with preparing a proposal detailing the scope and costs of the project. The committee, believing the project "would establish the university as a major center for Canadian–American research," stressed the importance of studies on state–provincial interactions to the growth of Canadian–American Studies and the recently established Pacific Northwest Studies Center which had a significant cross-border archival collection. The data center committee believed Western could eventually establish itself as *the* place known for research on state–provincial relations.[3] Initially, the primary focus of the data center would be on Washington state and British Columbia and then eventually be extended to include Alberta and Saskatchewan, and the states of Wyoming, Montana, Idaho, and Oregon. It was an ambitious proposal and certainly one that would require a significant cross-border infrastructure of personnel and computers, as well as a large amount of money. Scott's committee estimated start-up costs to be in the neighborhood of $50,000 and ongoing operational costs to be at least $250,000.

When Canadian government officials were asked to support the project they showed interest, but only if American co-funders could be found. As with most projects needing outside support,

Scott and his colleagues hoped to attract U.S. federal dollars. To this end, they cleverly thought naming the data center "The Warren G. Magnuson Center for Canadian–American Research" might help their cause by associating it with the prominent law maker. Magnuson, the highly influential senior U.S. Senator from Washington state, was the chairman of the powerful U.S. Senate Ways and Means Committee. His ability to direct federal dollars to various causes in the state was legendary. For years the University of Washington was one of the nation's top recipients of federal research grants—much of it owed to Magnuson's influence. The Senator's legacy is known today by the world class medical research facilities on, and surrounding, the University of Washington campus in Seattle. Western hoped some of this Magnuson magic might unleash federal dollars for the data center.

The data center proposal appealed to President Olscamp, who was determined to raise Western's research profile. Olscamp championed the idea in talks with officials at the Canadian Embassy and with members of the Washington state congressional delegation, including Senators Jackson and Magnuson. In a letter to James Colthart, the Academic Relations Officer at the Canadian Embassy, Olscamp said he was working to get support from Washington, D.C.

> I have spoken to Senators Jackson and Magnuson and our local congressman about the concept. All of them are enthusiastic. In fact, on a recent trip to Washington, Senator Jackson suggested that I use his good offices to set up an appointment with Premier Lougheed of Alberta to discuss the idea with him. Senator Jackson has given me his permission to inform Premier Lougheed that he, Jackson, is very interested in the idea. The time-table at this stage calls for me to bring a grant request for a pilot project, to include selected information about border transactions for British Columbia and the State of Washington to (Senator) Jackson at about this time next year.[4]

Despite Olscamp's efforts and at least the appearance of interest by Canadian and U.S. federal officials, including Senators Jackson and Magnuson, funding for the project was not realized.

Concerns were raised by Canadian officials that the maintenance needed to keep the data center timely would be costly and unpredictable. There were also uncertainties as to how commercial data would be handled. Additionally, data specialists expressed skepticism about how the venture would fare over time because the information technology revolution, already in full swing by the late 1970s, would likely diminish the value of the project in the future. In the end, what seemed like a promising addition to the Center and a valuable resource for Western could not generate enough federal interest on either side of the border to come to fruition.

Other program initiatives conceived in the late 1970s ran into various roadblocks, mostly because of lack of funding. The director was given a paltry .25 release time from his full teaching load. With budget reductions for state agencies and universities looming, there was little chance this would be increased. The Center was given a part-time secretary, clearly insufficient considering the increased scope of the program. Proposed student exchanges with nearby Simon Fraser University (SFU) in Burnaby and Capilano College in North Vancouver did not materialize, although a decade later in the early 1990s, an exchange program between Western and SFU finally happened.

The Canadian government was approached to fund faculty exchanges with Canadian universities, but it declined, saying this could not be done under the current grant guidelines. Instead, Canadian officials pushed the idea of a "government–scholars" exchange program where a federal civil servant would be appointed as a visiting scholar in Canadian–American Studies. That person, with practical experience within the Canadian government, could be used to give lectures and teach a course. In turn, a Canadian Studies faculty member—probably a member of the political science department—would be placed in a Canadian government agency as a visiting scholar. The idea, intriguing as it was, did not happen because of logistical complications and lack of faculty interest.

Beginning in 1977, Director Monahan began discussions with Ron Tallman, the director of the Canadian–American Center at the University of Maine, Orono, about creating a one-to-one Canadian

Studies faculty exchange between the two institutions.

In 1979, after lengthy correspondence, a committee composed of the directors and associate directors at both institutions met at St. Andrews, New Brunswick, to draw up an agreement. The terms were that one Canadian Studies scholar from each campus would be chosen to spend the fall term at the other's campus. The faculty member would teach one course, give public lectures and conduct a regional cross-border research project. The locations and foci of the two campuses—both situated in cross-border regions, with Maine's orientation to the New England–Atlantic Provinces–Québec region and Western's focus on British Columbia and the Pacific Northwest—made for parallel but quite different research and teaching settings.

Faculty members would be selected based on how the applicant's scholarly fields would benefit curricula, expansion of research in Canadian Studies, and student learning on each campus. An important part of the exchange would be a requirement that visiting professors interact with colleagues at nearby Canadian universities. Overall costs would be kept reasonable by requiring, where possible, that professors trade residences with one another and that they receive their regular salary from their home institution. Travel costs to Bellingham and Orono would be reimbursed, and up to $1,000 provided by each institution for research expenses. Faculty would also be given office space in each university's Canada House and have access to the resources of the host center.

While Western's administrators thought the exchange program would be valuable to the Center, pulling together the funding proved to be challenging. The dean of research thought the program would benefit teaching, but not research, and thus outside the purview of the research office. When the provost was approached for help, he sent a note to the president saying, "my office doesn't fund such activities." Undaunted, Center Director Monahan persevered and persuaded James Davis, dean of the College of Arts and Sciences, to make up the shortfall of just under $2,000. Davis wrote Monahan, "While this allocation puts this office in a tight corner, I feel that implementation of the Western–University of Maine Exchange

Agreement is so vital to the growth of our Canadian–American Studies program that I have mortgaged this office's 1979-80 budget to see this agreement through to completion."[5]

The WWU–Maine Faculty Exchange Program was launched and continued for 11 years, from 1980-1991. All told, 21 faculty members—11 from Western and 10 from Maine—participated. In most cases, residences were exchanged which added a personal dimension to the experience and reduced costs. Exchange faculty settled into offices in each Canadian Studies building (both programs happened to be located in former homes on campus) to facilitate mingling among colleagues.

The benefits of the exchange program were many. Some in particular stand out. First, most of the exchange professors offered courses on specialized topics from their home region which added something quite different to the curricula at the host institution. A few examples illustrate the point. Larry DeLorme, a professor of history at Western, taught a seminar at Maine titled, "Comparative Frontiers of the United States and Canada." Offering this course gave Maine students exposure to an aspect of North American history not available within the regular offerings of Maine's history department. David Sanger, University of Maine anthropology professor, taught "Prehistory of Northeast North America" through Western's anthropology department. Sanger's course, with its Northeastern focus, was a valuable complement to similar courses at Western on the Prehistory of the Pacific Northwest and Western Canada. I taught a course on Canadian Politics and Government that focused on Western Canada and particularly British Columbia. Western Canada was a world apart from Maine and the political science courses there focused more on the central and eastern parts of Canada and on the bordering provinces of Québec and New Brunswick.

Another benefit was the exchange program was an opportunity for faculty at both institutions to expand their research programs into a different Canada–U.S. cross-border region. David Sanger wrote, following his stay in Bellingham, that "the main reason for being on the West Coast was access to archaeologists and social anthropologists specializing in the anthropology in the area."

> The Northwest Coast Indian culture of Washington and B.C. was highly unusual, in its level of population density, social complexity and development of art and ritual. Because this culture flourished in the 19th century, it was reasonably well documented, unlike the east coast Indians whose culture was shattered before effective records were made."[6]

Exchanging residences simplified housing arrangements and provided a more community experience for the visiting faculty member. During my semester in Maine, our family lived in the Sanger's nineteenth century New England colonial home in Orono, located in a historical neighborhood a short walk from the university. The Sanger family, likewise, lived in our home in Bellingham. We were treated to Sanger's season tickets to attend the University of Maine Black Bears ice hockey games, joined with faculty and students on Saturday nights at Orono's famous Pat's Pizza and became friends with neighbors, most of whom had some connection to the university.

Indeed, the WWU–Maine Faculty Exchange Program had a positive impact on both Centers, and the faculty who participated. "I feel this is a most important opportunity to refresh and renew our faculty and to overcome the isolation of our geographical location," Monahan wrote to President Olscamp after concluding his own exchange semester in Orono in January 1981.[7] Western Provost James Talbot, who earlier had qualms about providing support for the WWU–Maine program, agreed with Monahan's sentiments who, after receiving written reports from faculty who had completed the exchange, penned a note to President G. Robert Ross (who had become president of Western in 1982) saying, "Bob, this is a fine exchange program."[8]

Tuition Reciprocity with British Columbia

An important goal of the Center was to develop faculty and student exchanges with other Canadian Studies programs, and especially with Canadian universities. The WWU–Maine Faculty Exchange Program was one way to advance this goal. But it was a faculty exchange and the partner institutions were located in the United States. Program leaders believed Canadian–American Studies students should experience Canada—preferably at a Canadian university—but also through direct interaction with Canadian students on campus.

Western always had a contingent of Canadian students, who mostly enrolled in programs not available in British Columbia such as speech pathology and audiology, and specialty programs in school administration. But Western students rarely attended Canadian universities. This seemed somewhat odd considering that British Columbia's two largest universities are located only about a 90-minute drive from Bellingham, within the cosmopolitan Vancouver area. Closeness was apparently viewed as sameness. For most Western students, study abroad meant going overseas to Europe, Australia or New Zealand, or some more distant locale. Making exchanges happen with a foreign country so geographically close to home proved to be no easy task.

In the mid-1970s, to encourage more British Columbia students to study at Western, and hopefully stimulate interest among Western and other Washington state students to study in Canada, university officials and several state legislators from legislative districts bordering Canada put forth an idea of a nonresident fee waiver agreement for students who wished to study in the other country. For Western's officials, the fee waiver idea was attractive because recruiting more Canadians would help maintain enrollment levels. But there was more to it than that. In the minds of some legislators, facilitating greater cross-border student exchange would strengthen cooperative ties between the state and province. Roger Van Dyken, a member of the Washington State House of Representatives from Bellingham and a supporter of the nonresident fee waiver, wrote: "we share the foundation of a common heritage which is sufficiently spiced with diversity to make increased cooperation and understanding mutually beneficial."[9]

The Center strongly supported the fee waiver for B.C. residents because having more Canadian students on campus would be a Canadian Studies educational force in its own right. The hope was that American students at Western would be encouraged to go north in higher numbers—a great way to encourage student exchanges with Canadian universities without having to work out separate bilateral college-to-college agreements, which were cumbersome to negotiate and required staff to manage.

In 1977, the Washington State Legislature enacted legislation to make the fee waiver idea a reality. It provided for B.C. students enrolled in undergraduate programs in any of the state's four-year institutions to pay the same tuition paid by in-state residents. The legislation stipulated that the arrangement would run until July 31, 1981, at which time state officials would review the program and make recommendations to the legislature as to whether it should be continued or terminated. British Columbia already allowed out-of-province students from both inside and outside Canada to pay the same tuition fees paid by B.C. residents. Thus, Washington legislature's action would offer a similar "reciprocity" to Canadian undergraduate students who pursued their studies in Washington state.

However, as early as spring 1980, signals were sent by state politicians that the tuition waiver agreement was not working because the net flow of students had been mostly southward.

Washington state's universities had accepted approximately ten Canadian students for each Washington student who chose to attend a Canadian university. State legislators expressed misgivings about the agreement because they saw it as Washington taxpayers subsidizing Canadian students.

William Chance, the head of the state's Council on Post-Secondary Education, the agency which managed the agreement, was an adamant supporter of reciprocity because, as he put it in a letter to Senator Warren Magnuson, "it would facilitate access for students in both jurisdictions, pave the way for longer-range programs of sharing—including academic planning, faculty exchanges, etc. and, in its own small way, contribute to the continued friendly relations between the neighboring countries.[10]

Aware that the state legislature was likely to end the program, President Olscamp and Chance, along with Western lobbyists and campus fiscal officials, set upon a strategy to seek federal funds to save the tuition waiver agreement. Chance argued that the matter of international exchanges should be seen as a federal concern. In a letter to Senator Magnuson, he explained his reasoning:

> The maintenance of friendly relations with Mexico and Canada is of paramount importance to the United States. Student exchange arrangements at the higher education level, through non-resident tuition waiver programs, are in the mutual benefit of each of the countries. Unfortunately, the individual states will not be able to afford to bear the full burden of such waivers. Moreover, if left to the development of the separate states, a consistent full border program will be unlikely. Since this is an area of enormous importance to this country, it would seem that a program reimbursing states willing to grant such waivers for a portion of the tuition loss would seem desirable.[11]

President Olscamp included Chance's thoughtful comments about federal funding of Canadian and Mexican student exchanges in his own letters to Senators Jackson and Magnuson, and Congressman Al Swift, who agreed to consider the request and discuss it with Magnuson. However, what became of the federal idea after Olscamp's request is unknown; no written record or further correspondence dealing with the matter could be found. What is known is that no federal funding was forthcoming and the fee waiver program would have to live or die depending on the will of the Washington State Legislature.

The state's higher education officials concluded their review of the fee waiver agreement in February 1981. The review recommended, with the support of Governor John Spellman, that the fee waiver program be continued until 1985 with a proviso that a more financially equitable arrangement be negotiated to recognize the imbalance of students between the state and province. The review noted that more than 1,500 students had participated in the program and the net "cost" to the State of Washington was $2.4 million. Also noted was that "only 32 Washington students had attended B.C. universities during this same period of time."[12] While there was some question as to the accuracy of these numbers, it was clear that many more B.C. students had benefitted from the program than Washington state students.

The review of the waiver agreement was only a recommendation. When the state legislature took up the matter, it voted to reject the review committee's finding and terminate the program. Considering the loss of tuition revenue for the state, the legislature's decision was not surprising. Washington State Speaker of the House, William M. Polk, probably spoke for most legislators when he wrote bluntly: "There was strong sentiment in the legislature that, in view of the state's financial situation, the money could be put to better use."[13]

Termination of the agreement meant Canadians already studying in Washington would have to pay out-of-state tuition, resulting in their fees increasing as much as 500 percent in the upcoming academic year. An attempt was made to pass "phase out" legislation allowing students currently affected by the agreement to finish their studies without a fee increase. Despite support for the measure by Western's president, legislators from Whatcom County, and the governor's office, the phase-out legislation failed to pass.

The reaction in British Columbia to Washington state's action was predictably negative. The *Vancouver Sun* published an editorial emblazoned with the title, "Bad Neighbors," which with unusual candor stated:

> This proposal in the name of budget cutting is pretty short-sighted on the part of Washington State officials. ... It will sour relations between neighbors. It is highly discriminatory. It will deny education to worthy students. It will drive away a Canadian presence in such institutions as Western Washington University which has some 260 students from B.C. It will narrow the outlook of the institution by denying American students the experience of cultural mingling with Canadians.[14]

For Washington lawmakers, the fiscal imbalance was the major reason for ending the agreement but it was not the only one. Spokane State Representative R.M. (Dick) Bond wrote to "remind" me—I was serving as acting director of the Center at the time—that the cost of university instruction to the taxpayer is far more than what is paid in in-state tuition. He wrote, "taxpayers in this state still subsidize parts of the cost for nonresidents" (referring to Canadians). He then took umbrage at the *Vancouver Sun's* editorial:

> I must point out that Canada has a lot more damage to repair than we do. The greed and extortion which has characterized their natural gas export policy has resulted in every natural gas consumer in the State of Washington paying more than 60 percent of his gas bill in the form of Canadian taxes. The only reason advanced is that they don't want to sell for less than the Arabs do. That is why they are known as blue-eyed Arabs. ... You may forward this letter to the Vancouver Sun if you wish. I strongly suggest you turn your studies in this direction.[15]

Bond's comment revealed a level of animosity toward Canada for its gas export policy that still lingered within some legislative circles, despite the feelings of goodwill expressed by many lawmakers who supported tuition reciprocity. Clearly, the bilateral political environment was still in need of some repair if there was to be progress in reducing tuition for Canadians studying in Washington state.

The termination of the fee waiver agreement coincided with a cut in the Center's budget—a 10 percent reduction in 1982. These hits taken by the program prompted Helen Groh, the recently appointed Canadian Consul in Seattle, to ask Director Monahan in December 1981 whether Western still had the same commitment to Canadian–American Studies. President Olscamp found it necessary to write the consulate explaining that state financial circumstances had caused some setbacks but "the university's commitment to the program and to things Canadian remains unchanged."[16]

A tuition waiver program for Canadians wanting to attend Washington state universities was dead, but it resurfaced in an altered form some 10 years later. In 1993, agreements were signed between Washington state and two- and four-year institutions in

British Columbia creating a much scaled-back tuition waiver program. Essentially a program based on quotas, the 1993 agreement provided for 33 university slots in Washington to be available to Canadians at equivalent in-state resident rates and divided among the state's four-year institutions. Of the 33 slots available, Western held 18. Canadian students would have to compete for the slots, with priority given to those applying for degree programs that were unavailable in their home country. This limitation significantly limited who was eligible and weakened the "cultural mingling" element of the exchange concept.

In 1999, with program numbers dwindling and interest waning, the Washington–British Columbia agreement ended. The idea that cross-border reciprocity agreements in higher education would facilitate cultural diversity and contribute to greater understanding of each country was largely abandoned.

The Battle for Canada House

Canada House was an important part of the Center's development. A separate building on campus dedicated to Canadian–American Studies signified that Western was indeed a place where teaching and research on Canada was strongly supported and appreciated. The house itself—a heritage building perched on a campus hillside overlooking Bellingham Bay and Southwest British Columbia—symbolized the importance of Canada to both Western and the state. However, Canada House was also a part of Western's physical space infrastructure and, like other offices, the facility was institutional space given to one program and not others.

From the time Canada House was assigned to the Center, other groups had designs on the building. It was prime space from a location standpoint and the fact that it was not a typical institutional building added to its appeal. With multiple bedrooms serving as office space and downstairs dining and living areas ideal for receptions and small seminars, the multifunctional building was clearly an ideal facility for programs that existed outside of colleges or regular academic departments. Canadian–American Studies initially was assigned the downstairs part of the building with the Center for Pacific Northwest Studies' archival collection consigned to the upper floor, the basement and the back porch. This was a more or less compatible use of space, and the arrangement was acceptable to both parties for a time.

In 1982, a group of faculty and administrators formed Western's first Faculty Club. The Faculty Club at Western, like those at other universities, was conceived as a place where faculty, senior-level administrators and their guests could interact outside the normal campus environment, usually over drinks, meals and during social events. Western's Faculty Club described its purposes as "of a social, academic, philanthropic and professional nature." Membership would be open to all faculty with at least half-time appointments and to senior level administrators. Fees were set at $25 to join with dues of $5 per month. Regular staff personnel were not eligible to join the club, a rule which, shortly after the club opened, prompted a protest by Ruth Schooner, a member of the chemistry department clerical staff, who "crashed" one of the club's Friday social hours. Likely influenced by Schooner's action, the club was soon open to all Western employees.[17] The club's weekly activities, according to its charter, would include a daily luncheon and a Friday afternoon social gathering over beer, wine and cocktails. Further, the club would conduct special programs such as quarterly speaker forums and occasional dinner events.

Needing space for the new venture, the leaders of the Faculty Club cast their eyes on Canada House. Joining forces with the university's Retirement Association, they made their wishes known:

> The WWU Faculty Club and Retirement Association propose that Canada House be set aside as their "home" on a permanent basis, and that Canada House be jointly occupied by these organizations.[18]

While this action had all the trappings of a hostile takeover from the point of view of Canadian–American Studies, the Faculty Club proposal acknowledged that the current occupants of Canada House couldn't just be kicked out, but needed to be accommodated. Mindful of this, the proposal stated that two issues needed "administrative assistance and input." The first was; could Canadian–American Studies "remain [in Canada House] with reduced office space?" The second was; could Canadian–American Studies "be assured of gaining equal or better office/academic space," should the Center be required to move out of Canada House?[19] While perhaps a good faith effort to work with the Center, the idea that the Faculty Club could simply bully its way into the building was objectionable to program faculty and others, many of whom were in favor of a new Faculty Club on campus, but not happy about it being located in Canada House.

The Faculty Club's organizational meeting was held in a large classroom on May 26, 1982, to make the club official. About 75 faculty and administrators attended the meeting, most of whom supported the formation of the Faculty Club and its proposed move into Canada House. Some faculty at the meeting with little or no connection to Canadian–American Studies were in favor of the club but let it be known that it was wrong for a nonacademic entity to displace an academic program. Center Director Monahan, speaking at the meeting, said he had long agreed about the need for a Faculty Club on campus, but opposed its move into Canada House because he believed the club was incompatible with an academic unit and, moreover, if it was located there, it would seek to take over the whole building as its membership grew. President Olscamp, who was a key force for locating Canadian–American Studies in Canada House in the first place, told the meeting he now was, as he put it, "a charter member" of the Faculty Club and he insisted that placing the club in Canada House would not expel any academic program. Although these pronouncements did not dispel the concerns expressed by Monahan and many colleagues, the strong support for the club—especially by administrators—made it all but inevitable that the Faculty Club would get approval to move into Canada House.

However, before the necessary administrative endorsements were in place, the matter of how the new club would be financed came under scrutiny, particularly from students working on the campus newspaper—*The Western Front*. At issue was whether or not an exclusive Faculty Club would be self-supporting or draw funds from university sources. Administrative officials, including Olscamp, defended the club's financial plan, declaring that dues from the members would cover costs of rent, furnishings and social events, thus insisting no university dollars—including student funds—would be used.

On June 4, the *Bellingham Herald* reported that students had lodged a protest against the club, claiming that state money was being improperly used to support a non-university activity. As reported in the *Herald*, "the Faculty Club finds itself in the midst of a controversy over whether student fees or taxpayers' money will wind up helping to pay for professors' socializing."[20] The students learned that architectural drawings for Faculty Club renovations of Canada House had already been made and paid for by the university, so they were correct in their charge of improper use of university money.

The University Facilities Committee, charged with approving the allocation of space on campus, upon learning of the students concerns, voted to stop the Faculty Club's move to Canada House until the financial and legal issues could be resolved. Some on the committee had other worries as well, in particular, what the change to Canada House might say about the school's dedication to Canadian–American Studies and whether, as one committee member put it, a weakened commitment "might affect relations with Canada."[21]

The committee's action only delayed the approval process. In the end, the power of the upper administration and fairly strong support from the faculty for the takeover of Canada House eventually carried the day. Objections about improper use of student tuition and state funds to support the club were allayed—many would say swept under the rug—by the university's legal office, and by the time classes resumed in fall quarter, the UFC and the Board of Trustees had approved the club and its occupancy of Canada House. With 165 initial members, the club officially began operations with a Canada House grand opening on October 1, 1982.

Now sharing space with the Faculty Club, Canadian–American Studies was moved to the upper floor and "guaranteed exclusive use of that floor." An agreement was struck with the club's leaders that gave Canadian Studies events "priority use" of downstairs meeting space when the Faculty Club was closed. The meaning of "priority use" was never clearly determined and overall management of the downstairs space was put under the jurisdiction of the Office of Continuing Education and Conferences, which almost immediately started renting out Canada House's first floor to outside groups during evenings and weekends to generate revenue. The remaining tenant in the building, the Center for Pacific Northwest Studies, was relocated to the commissary building on the southside of campus, a move that pleased director James Scott as he feared that a fire in Canada House—an increased possibility in an old house now being used as an eatery and cocktail lounge—would destroy the center's archival collection.

The new arrangement, perhaps the best that Canadian–American Studies could get, was never a happy one. It didn't help that even before the final approvals for the Faculty Club had been signed, club leaders took matters into their own hands to rid the downstairs of Canadian–American Studies. While Director Monahan was away during the early part of the summer, his downstairs office was dismantled and moved in pieces upstairs. When Monahan returned, he found that his books and bookshelves were just dumped in a mound on the floor in his new upstairs office. As Monahan later told me, when he walked into his office and saw the pile of books, he was so outraged that he kicked the metal wastebasket from one end of the office to the other, smashing it like a squashed tin can. The club members apologized but their callous action further inflamed what could best be called a tense relationship between the Center and the Faculty Club

It was obvious from the outset that the functions of the Canadian–American Studies academic program and the Faculty Club were incompatible. The lunch operation left the building filled with unpleasant food odors that lingered late in the day after the club was closed. The Canadian–American Studies staff secretary, who had an office at the top of the stairs, complained to university health officials that the lack of proper ventilation was making her ill. The building was an old house, not a restaurant, and it did not have a proper ventilation system. The university did nothing to improve the air quality and the response from the Faculty Club's caterers was to open the downstairs kitchen windows wider. The building was rented out on weekends for events, including wedding receptions and other non-university functions. On many Monday mornings, Canadian–American Studies staff were greeted with garbage in the kitchen, sticky floors from spilled drinks and the lingering smell of cigarette smoke. Over time, nothing much changed, despite continuing complaints from Canada House personnel over several years.

Acting Program Director James Hitchman, filling in for Monahan while he was on sabbatical, wrote in 1988, "food aromas, radio noise and dining people do not harmonize with office routine, writing research and meetings."[22] Hitchman, in his efforts to persuade university officials to relocate the Faculty Club, noted how the Center was expanding and needed more space, not less. He pointed to the need for an office for research faculty, a seminar room for meetings and classes, and space to display and store materials for the growing teacher outreach programs. As he noted, sharing the building with the Faculty Club also detracted from the important diplomatic functions conducted at Canada House. Hitchman outlined the issues:

> Many dignitaries and officials visit Canada House and the way upstairs is not very pleasant. This is an internationally recognized program where government officials, academicians, businessman and others from several foreign nations stop and spend time… It is not easy to solicit funds from premiers, governors and executive officers out of a shabby garret. Diplomatic and consular officials are merely polite and sympathetic when they meet here. It would be good hospitality and smart politics to offer a better physical setting.[23]

The Center was persistent, if not terribly successful, in its efforts over several years to persuade administrative officials and key faculty committees to return Canada House to its academic function. It turned out to be a contest that pitted a small, interdepartmental program against Faculty Club members, many of whom were university administrators, who could see no good reason why Canadian–American Studies needed the whole building or, for that matter, could not be moved to other departmental or administrative space. On one occasion, one of Western's provosts confided to me that although he agreed in principle with the Center's case, he was "not about to get into a fight with faculty over this issue."

The Faculty Club remained in Canada House for 22 years, although the attendance at luncheons gradually declined to the point where hiring caterers was no longer feasible. The university was changing and younger faculty spent less time on campus and generally were not interested in being part of a social club. The Friday afternoon cocktail parties continued, much to the chagrin of some campus officials who thought the boozy affairs were inviting calamity on the roads and serious liability problems for the university.

By 2015, the Faculty Club, with declining membership and a makeshift approach to catering the Friday afternoon drinking sessions, was relocated to the Viking Union, the main campus food services building. The Center for Canadian–American Studies finally regained control of Canada House and it became home to a new configuration of programs called Canada House Programs.

6
National Recognition

Reaching Out

In the 1980s, free trade became the dominant issue in Canada–U.S. relations when Prime Minister Brian Mulroney and President Ronald Reagan began negotiations on the Canada–U.S. Free Trade Agreement. As part of the Center's mission of delving into international policy issues, several forums were held to examine regional impacts and implications of expanded Canada–U.S. trade.

Some of these events resulted in direct policy actions, the most important being the PACE (Peace Arch Crossing Entry) program that created a separate car lane for frequent border crossers at the Blaine Port of Entry, the main passenger vehicle entry point between Washington and British Columbia. The idea for PACE was first discussed in Canada House on January 26, 1989, at a forum involving regional planners, business leaders and academics. PACE was designed to help speed the flow of passenger vehicles across the border at a time when both car and truck traffic was rapidly increasing. People who enrolled in the PACE program would have a sticker affixed to their car windshield that allowed them use of a special lane when crossing the border. When rolled out in 1992, PACE and its Canada counterpart, CANPASS (for Canadians crossing into the United States), were unique along the entire Canada–U.S. border. PACE and CANPASS were the precursors to the current NEXUS trusted traveler program, begun after 9/11, that allows prescreened travelers expedited border crossing in dedicated NEXUS car lanes. It is significant that Canadian–American Studies faculty—particularly economists—working with other organizations in Whatcom County and Seattle, provided research and ongoing consultation on the workings of these programs. This working relationship between the Center and policy officials to improve traffic flow at the border would intensify with the creation of the Border Policy Research Institute at Western in 2005.

In 1986, the American Assembly, a prestigious public policy think-tank founded in 1950 by Dwight D. Eisenhower and based at Columbia University in New York, tapped Western to hold a conference focused on Canada–U.S. relations. The American Assembly was well known nationally for bringing leaders in government and academe together to generate new ideas for solving policy problems. Two years earlier in November, 1984, the American Assembly convened a major conference in Washington, D.C., on Canada–U.S. Relations. Western was selected to host a follow-up meeting to assess bilateral issues of particular relevance to the West Coast.

The conference was held at Sudden Valley, a woodsy lakeside resort community located about 10 miles from Bellingham on Lake Whatcom. Coincidentally, Canadians were a majority of Sudden Valley recreational property holders, many who lived full time in the nearby Vancouver metro area. Conference speakers discussed the need for greater bilateral cooperation on environmental, energy, trade and cultural issues. The latter involved Canada's efforts to protect its cultural industries—communication media, artists and writers—from being overwhelmed by American TV, periodicals, movies, books, and artistic work that flooded into Canada. The issue had particular relevance locally because KVOS Television, a Bellingham station, developed a cross-border business model where they geared programming to a large audience in Southwest British Columbia. The situation irked many Canadians because B.C. businesses would advertise on the Bellingham station, thus diverting advertising revenue away from local broadcasters. Even more bothersome for Canadians worried about the erosion of Canadian culture, KVOS was filling air time in British Columbia with American

TV shows. The Canadian government responded by taking actions intended to make it economically unfeasible for KVOS to broadcast in what had become its prime market in Canada. The issue demonstrated an important difference between the two countries. Many, if not most Canadians accept government actions such as tax policy and regulatory measures to protect home grown cultural industries (TV programming being an important one) from foreign influence. This contrasts with the strong propensity in the U.S. to allow the marketplace to determine cultural development at home and throughout the world. Of course with the U.S. being so dominant a cultural force globally, Americans pay little or no attention to such things.

The conference issued a report stating that the Canada–U.S. relationship was strong, but always "vulnerable to small disagreements growing into larger problems." Many of these "small disagreements" were especially important on the West Coast: Canada's policies on oil and gas exports to the U.S; enduring Canada–U.S. disputes over regional lumber exports and salmon allocations; environmental concerns about oil traffic in the Puget Sound and Strait of Georgia; and the protection of a Canadian cultural industry. With these issues in mind, conferees called for a bilateral commission to examine protectionism, promote more cooperation on environmental issues and create a joint Canada–U.S. research program to support the work of negotiators and scientists under the Pacific Salmon Treaty. As important as the report was, probably the most significant conference outcome was increasing participants' awareness of cross-border issues in the West, often ignored or misunderstood by Eastern-centric officials and academics who dominated the foreign policy establishments in both countries. Another outcome, according to reports from Bellingham real estate agents, was a surge of property buying in Sudden Valley by out of state visitors impressed with the natural beauty of the area.

The Center's heightened focus on political and business outreach in the cross-border region prompted interest in student internships aimed at providing experiential learning in Canada. State and provincial governments, trade associations and the federal consulates in Seattle and Vancouver were viewed as targets of opportunity. In particular, we set our sights on creating a joint B.C.–Washington legislative internship program where students would do internships in both the state legislature in Olympia, Washington, and the legislative assembly in the provincial capital in Victoria, B.C. Western, through its political science department, already had a well-established student internship program in the Washington State Legislature, and UBC had a similar program in the B.C. Legislature. State and provincial officials advised us that the best course of action would be to piggyback on these existing programs. This looked to be easy until we learned that the political science departments at UBC and Western, not wanting to disrupt settled programs, were not interested in grafting on to their legislative internships the hoped-for "two capital" intern experience contemplated by the Center. What was an exciting learning opportunity, seemingly within our grasp, faltered on all-to-common institutional resistance that so often hinders cross-border academic projects.

We were more successful placing interns on an ad hoc basis in government and business offices including the Washington State Office of Trade and Development, the Consulates General in Seattle and Vancouver, and Washington state companies doing business with Canada. Even here, problems arose such as whether or not a Western student interning in Canada was actually "working" and therefore subject to immigration laws pertaining to foreign workers.

The Center's K–12 Study Canada outreach saw considerable expansion during the 1980s. The numbers of teachers attending the summer institutes from outside Washington soon exceeded those from inside the state. Some former alums of the program were appointed as "teacher associates" to conduct mini-Study Canada workshops in their school districts out of state. This enabled the Center to get curriculum materials in the hands of more teachers, particularly in states like Oregon, Colorado and Arizona, where cohorts of teachers interested in Canada began to develop.

K–12 Study Canada was gradually becoming national in geographic scope. The content taught also changed. Shifting from its beginnings as mostly a Washington state-based program heavily focused on regional subject matter, Study Canada now incorporated nontraditional topics such as environmental and transportation problems in North America, Canadian art and literature and Indigenous peoples. One noteworthy event was linking the Study Canada Summer Institute with the EXPO 86 World's Fair in Vancouver, B.C., that occurred over five months in the summer of 1986. Two Study Canada teacher programs were held that summer which incorporated trips to the EXPO 86 site to take advantage of the exposition's learning programs. Though tourist attractions were the biggest part of the fair, outstanding educational programs easily adaptable for classroom use were integrated into the main exposition, themed to transportation and communication, with focus on subjects like polar transportation, alternative fuel and power systems, and the importance of large-scale transportation systems in the evolution of modern Canada. The 40 Study Canada teachers (20 in each institute) happily took advantage of these resources to augment Canadian content in their teaching materials, while enjoying a very popular world's fair.

In 1987, the Center joined with other faculty in the region to form the Pacific Northwest Canadian Studies Consortium (PNWCSC), an organization of more than 25 universities and colleges in the Pacific Northwest states, British Columbia and Alberta. The founding meeting, held at the University of Washington, gathered together faculty from Western, UW and the University of Oregon. The idea for a region-wide Canadian Studies consortium was the brainchild of University of Oregon professor Bryan Downes who believed the growing number of Canadian Studies groups in the region, both large and small, needed to be more closely linked together. To this end, the consortium was envisioned as a kind of clearing house for Canadian Studies information about faculty, course syllabi, bibliographies and grant opportunities. It also began an annual faculty development workshop held annually at sites in provinces and territories in Western Canada. Western's Center organized the initial workshop at Royal Roads Military College near Victoria in August 1988.

In following years, similar workshops were held in Haida Gwaii

(Formerly the Queen Charlotte Islands), Calgary, Edmonton, Whitehorse (Yukon), the B.C. Okanagan region and Victoria. Eventually, the PNWCSC workshops, always involving faculty visits to Canadian universities, were organized by Kevin Cook, the academic and public affairs officer at the Canadian Consulate General in Seattle.

These activities in consort with the Center's expanding curriculum were important in positioning Western as an emerging leader in Canadian Studies in the United States during the 1980s. However, challenges, as always, were considerable. As usual, new funding sources would be needed to maintain and expand the teaching, research and outreach functions of the program. State funded university budgets, supplemented by relatively small grants from Canada's Understanding Canada program and occasionally from foundations and businesses simply could not provide enough money for the kind of nonconventional program that had developed. Nor could the Center, a loose interdepartmental grouping of faculty in a highly departmentalized university, expect to effectively compete for scarce university resources. Center Acting Director James Hitchman, in a 1988 report to the president, quipped that "we are trying to fly a B-17 with a Spad engine."[1] Seeking federal dollars through various U.S. Department of Education programs was one hopeful avenue. Another was to embark on a campaign for significant non-university funding to support dedicated faculty positions in Canadian–American Studies. Both avenues would be pursued.

A National Resource Center

For the long term, the Center's main objective was to add more faculty to fill gaps in the curriculum and strengthen the teaching program. The Center did not have any faculty positions of its own and with tight state budgets there was virtually no prospect the university would provide any. The hope was that outside money, most likely from the federal government, could be found to fund dedicated Canadian Studies faculty positions. This was the top priority when the Center made its first application for federal funding under the National Defense Education Act (NDEA) Title VI National Resource Centers program in 1984, and in subsequent submissions thereafter.

In 1958 at the height of the Cold War, the federal government enacted the NDEA to provide funding to U.S. universities to help them develop foreign language and area studies programs. The NDEA was inspired by government officials' national security concerns about the lack of expertise on "critical world areas" in schools, universities and in the foreign policy bureaucracy of the federal government. At its outset, the program focused on the Soviet Union, Eastern Europe, East Asia and Africa, areas in which there was a profound deficiency in Americans' knowledge of languages, history and political and cultural dynamics. Federal funding under the NDEA program was used to create National Resource Centers (NRCs) at competitively selected universities for the purpose of language training, undergraduate and graduate teaching, and research focused on these world areas. Universities receiving funding to create NRCs were also required to develop training programs for teachers in American elementary and secondary schools and community colleges to equip them to be proficient in history, politics, social dynamics and languages in these same areas of the world.

Canada, with its traditional close ties to the United States, was viewed by the government as outside the realm of Cold War politics of the 1950s and 1960s and was not included in the NDEA program in its early years. The situation changed in the 1970s when the NDEA's scope was expanded to include Canada and Latin America. U.S. Senator Mike Gravel of Alaska led the effort in the U.S Senate to bring Canada into the program, arguing that Canada was not only a country of rapidly increasing importance to the U.S., but a "distinct country about which most Americans are insufficiently knowledgeable."

Duke University and Michigan State University were the first higher education institutions to receive grants under NDEA—known as Title VI funding—to further develop their Canadian

Studies programs. This group expanded in 1979 when the University of Maine, with one of the oldest Canadians Studies programs in the U.S., partnered with the University of Vermont and was granted Title VI funding. Eventually, The State University of New York at Plattsburgh (SUNY–Plattsburgh) was added as a third member to the Maine-led consortium. This coveted Title VI status provided significant federal dollars to the Canadian Studies programs at these universities to expand their activities and to help them compete for other private and government funding.

Becoming a National Resource Center was a long-time goal of Western's Center. However, as a non-Ph.D. granting institution, the university needed to partner with a major research university to be eligible. The Center could have applied for federal grant funding under the Department of Education's Undergraduate Areas Studies Centers' program, but these grants were considerably smaller and shorter term than those received by NRCs. When Center Director Monahan and his colleagues sized up the situation, they decided a consortium arrangement partnering Western with one or more West Coast universities with Canadian Studies programs would offer the best chance to secure federal funding under the NDEA program.

In September 1984, Western hosted a planning meeting to create a Canadian Studies consortium that would apply for NDEA funding. Canadian Studies directors in attendance were from the University of Washington (Douglas Jackson), the University of Southern California (Michael Fry), Simon Fraser University (Parzival Copes) and Western Washington University (Robert Monahan). Others at the meeting were Donald Wilson, a UBC professor of education who had helped develop Western's K–12 Study Canada program, Steven Lamy, the director of public education in international affairs at USC, and myself, the Center's associate director. The planning group agreed to form a three-university consortium and prepare a request for a Canadian Studies area grant under NDEA Title VI National Resource Centers for International Studies, 1985–87. The three American universities, USC, UW and Western, would be the consortium partners, and

Simon Fraser University, because it was outside the United States—and thus ineligible to receive U.S. federal dollars—would have "affiliate status to provide support for various activities undertaken by the consortium."[2] By all accounts, the University of Washington, by virtue of its location in the Pacific Northwest and experience running a Canadian Studies program, was the logical campus to serve as the lead institution for the consortium. However, UW Canadian Studies Director Douglas Jackson had other responsibilities that would take him away from Seattle that fall making him unable to fully participate in the preparation of the grant proposal. As a result, Michael Fry accepted the responsibility to be the principal investigator for the NRC grant, thus positioning USC as the consortium lead university.

An obvious question was why create a consortium of universities that would stretch 1,300 miles from the Canadian border to Los Angeles? The answer was that the NRC was intended as a "West Coast Center" with a different orientation from the others located in the upper Midwest, in the Northeast and at Duke University in North Carolina. The planning group discussed the need for western perspectives in research and teaching because of the traditional dominance of eastern centers of political and economic power. And, the group wanted to ensure that input from the entire Pacific West would be incorporated in the consortium. The three universities, because of geography and specialized studies, could bring different, but complementary expertise and perspectives on the West and Canada. USC, with its strength in international relations and trade, would bring to the NRC its teaching and research on Canada's trade ties with California and the Pacific Rim. The University of Washington's professional schools would add expertise on fisheries, forestry and environmental science, all major areas of importance in Canada–U.S. relations in the West. Another strength at the UW was its groundbreaking programs in Indigenous languages and culture, including those about the Canadian Arctic region. Western Washington University had one of the strongest undergraduate programs in Canadian Studies in the nation and it was a leader in the development of K–12 curriculum materials on Canada written from a West Coast perspective. USC's Steven Lamy, a specialist in social studies curriculum, had collaborated with Western on its K–12 Study Canada project in earlier years, including hosting a Study Canada summer institute at the USC campus in Los Angeles.

A Canadian Studies NRC with an entire West Coast focus had appeal. But could it work with more than 1,000 miles separating the lead university from the others? How could the NRC perform basic functions such as sharing faculty, exchanging students, holding regular meetings and conducting joint workshops and conferences? Officials in the Department of Education in Washington, D.C., had hinted that the project was probably too ambitious and that it would make more sense for Western and the University of Washington to create a two-university consortium. It was certainly true that Canadian Studies was much more developed in the Pacific Northwest than in Los Angeles, and the UW's Henry M. Jackson School of International Studies already housed six NRC Title VI area studies centers. A Canadian Studies NRC would be a natural addition.

We had a good sense of the challenge and the poor odds of success when we wrote and submitted the proposal in the fall of 1984. We had a seriousness of purpose, but also a "nothing to lose"—even a casual—attitude as we went about the task of preparing the application. One of the grant preparation sessions, held in Bellingham on a Saturday at the Lakewood boathouse on Lake Whatcom, a property owned by Western, was productive but also rushed so the USC contingent (Fry and Lamy) could get back to the hotel to watch the USC Trojans football game. Another session was held at the Canadian Consulate General office in Seattle. Fry flew up from Los Angeles and made it clear that most, if not all, of the work needed to be done in one day. My memory of the session is of Fry, not wanting to waste time with outlines or time-consuming discussion, reciting proposal language and me frantically typing as he talked.

Once completed, the proposal did not seem compelling. Everyone knew the distance between the schools was a huge liability and no amount of justification could overcome this fact. More important were substantive problems. The lack of Canadian specialists, courses and faculty and almost no administrative commitment to Canadian Studies at USC could not be papered over. The comments from grant reviewers clearly revealed this weakness. Summarizing these shortcomings, an official from the Department of Education said:

> Reviewers said that a Canadian center on the West Coast is sorely needed. WWU is strong at the undergraduate level; USC has some leading scholars in IR [international relations]—but severe weaknesses are evident. Commitment at USC is weak; padding of courses is obvious...[3]

I doubt if anyone involved in the consortium was surprised when the Department of Education rejected the grant proposal. The question of what to do next was now on the table. The answer was obvious: Western and the UW should go it alone. The next grant competition occurred in 1986 and the two Pacific Northwest universities teamed up, with UW director Douglas Jackson assuming the lead role. From a curricular and geography standpoint, a UW–WWU consortium was attractive and workable. Western's undergraduate strength and UW's graduate and professional school assets formed a logical division of labor and a natural pathway for students to move from undergraduate work at Western to graduate studies at the UW. The distance between the campuses was relatively close (about 85 miles), and Seattle and Bellingham had strong regional ties with British Columbia. Joining forces became even more compelling when the program officer at the Department of Education who managed the Title VI programs strongly encouraged Monahan and Jackson to work together. There was some thought about keeping USC as a partner and forming a three-way consortium again, but Department of Education officers in Washington, D.C., advised against this approach.

The new effort paid off as the UW–WWU consortium proposal was funded. Reviewers found both schools to have solid strengths in most facets of Canadian Studies, and saw huge potential in the Pacific Northwest, where they believed Canadian Studies was at its strongest in the West. Leadership was seen as a big plus. The directors of the two consortium institutions, both geographers, were not only professional colleagues but also long-time friends, which helped with handling the endless detail of grant management made more complicated by being intertwined in two different university systems. The administrative structure of the NRC was based at UW, but Western as a subcontractor controlled its own budget and spending. As the lead institution, the UW initially received a larger percentage of the grant dollars. The two universities eventually agreed to a 50-50 split of the total funds received, a fair yet generous arrangement given the disproportionate size of the two institutions.

USC continued to build its Canadian program within its School for International Relations, emphasizing the international dimensions of Canadian Studies. USC's Steve Lamy retained his ties with Western's K–12 curriculum program. SFU did not play any official role in the UW–WWU consortium, although Western's faculty worked with SFU colleagues in many ways—hosting speakers and visiting lecturers, instituting student exchanges, and collaborating on research. Our partner at UBC, Don Wilson, continued to be a key player in all matters relating to K–12 curriculum development for the new UW–WWU consortium for many years.

Western's top priority in the new grant was a tenure-track position in economics. A way would have to be found to fund it over the long term since Title VI funding was limited to a 3-year grant cycle. With the provost's blessing, we wrote into the grant a cost-sharing plan where federal funding would support one-half of the position salary for three years, with the proviso that Western would provide the other half, and then assume full funding for the position after the end of three years. Western's provost, Larry DeLorme, signed off on the funding arrangement and in future grants the same cost sharing formula was used to create three additional faculty positions in French, geography and environmental studies. That the administration agreed to this scheme was a sign of commitment to the program by the provost, although DeLorme at one point, apparently not remembering he had approved the grants, said he had been "rolled" and later told me in no uncertain terms that any new Canadian Studies positions in departments leveraged by the Center's federal grants would be limited to the duration of the grants unless they were prioritized through the university's overall planning process.

An economics position fully focused on Canada was a crucial building block for the Center. For the first time, courses on the Canadian economy became a permanent part of the Canadian Studies curriculum. This was all the more important because during this time (late 1980s) bilateral trade ties were receiving more attention in Canada–U.S. relations than ever before, only to increase after the advent of the Canada–U.S. Free Trade Agreement in 1988. And, the timing was opportune because the new Canadian economics position coincided with the creation of a new endowed professorship in Canada–U.S. business and economic relations.

Creating an Endowed Professorship

In the mid-1980s, the Washington State Legislature established a trust fund to support a small number of special [also referred to as "distinguished"] professorships at universities throughout the state. The aim of the program was to strengthen the state's public four-year institutions by adding special professorships made possible through partnerships between citizens and the campuses. Through a matching grant program, the state would help universities create endowments for funding these professorships. A university could apply for $250,000 from the special professorships' fund conditioned on the institution matching the state funds with an equal amount of private or other non-state money. The proceeds of the endowment could be used to supplement the professor's salary, to pay salaries for her assistants, and to pay expenses associated with the professor's scholarly work. Universities normally would be limited to one special professorship. Campuses would decide internally which position to put forth, potentially setting up a competition for the professorship within each university. The guidelines called for the positions to be senior level with commensurate base salaries provided by the university.

Center Director Robert Monahan, never one to overlook an opportunity to grow the program, approached the College of Business and Economics with the idea of a distinguished professorship in Canada–U.S. business and economic relations. With growing national and regional interest in Canada–U.S. trade, Monahan believed the position would be a natural fit for Western with its expanding Canadian–American Studies program. Practically speaking, the professorship would be a valuable resource for both education on Canada–U.S. economic ties, and for fostering cooperation on regional cross-border business and economic affairs between the two countries. As Monahan wrote, "we believe this professorship would be the CENTERPIECE of the university's new initiatives in cooperative interregional economic development, international trade and Pacific Rim Marketing"[4]

It was envisioned that the holder of the distinguished professorship would be a person of considerable accomplishment in academe, government or business. In addition to teaching courses in the individual's area of expertise, the professor would be expected to speak frequently to off-campus business and government groups, guest lecture at Western as well as other colleges and universities in the region, and organize occasional conferences to address timely issues. Because business relationships between the two countries are dynamic, it was decided that the position should be short term—Monahan proposed three years maximum—to ensure a continuing inflow of new ideas and perspectives in the professorship as economic relations between the two countries inevitably changed over time. The focus of the professorship and the short term, rotational principle that would guide duration of appointments were all formulated in a proposal which the university accepted and submitted to the state as Western's application for the Washington state special professorship program.

Monahan found strong supporters for the distinguished professorship in Alan Rowe, the Consul at the Canadian Consulate General in Seattle and Richard Seaborn, a Canadian career diplomat with extensive experience in Ottawa. Both liked the idea of a business and economics professorship dedicated to Canadian Studies that would "rotate" new people into the position every few years. Rowe and Seaborn promised to work their connections in the Canadian federal government to help in any way they could.

As it turned out, the Canadian government's help was more crucial than was first thought. To receive the state funding for the professorship, $250,000 in matching money would be needed. Monahan's early fund-raising efforts turned up few propects. The Western Foundation, the university's private fundraising arm, agreed to be a donor but did not want to be responsible for the full amount. With the consulate's help and encouragement from officials in Ottawa, a plan was devised to ask the Canadian federal government for a $250,000 grant to be used as matching money to secure the $250,000 from the state professorship fund. Officials in the Department of External Affairs in Ottawa were pleased with Western's success in developing a strong undergraduate program in Canadian Studies, liked the professorship's focus on economics and business and they had a great deal of confidence in Monahan. Plans were made for Monahan to travel to Ottawa to meet with Canadian Department of External Affairs officials, to whom he would make the case for the professorship and the needed money. Canadian officials insisted that the president of Western, G. Robert Ross, also go to Ottawa to signify the university's commitment. Ross agreed, and the Ottawa meetings, which included Canadian officials from several government departments and academics from the University of Ottawa, were set for July 15, 1987.

The Western contingent, booked into the impressive Chateau Laurier Hotel, received the royal treatment from their Canadian hosts. After meetings over two days, Monahan and Ross left the Canadian capital feeling reasonably confident the requested funding would be forthcoming. As it turned out, Canadian federal officials pledged $100,000 toward the $250,000 needed to receive the state match, conditioned on Western supplying more information on how the professorship would be used, the rationale for short term appointments, and the remaining fundraising strategy including specific donor targets. Once approved, the Canadian money would be paid in one-third increments over three years. Monahan commented later that he thought he had failed by not convincing the Canadian government to pledge the full $250,000. President Ross reassured him the trip was successful because, in his view, a significant commitment had been made by the Government of Canada that would make fundraising for the additional $150,000 easier.

Even before the trip to Ottawa, Monahan had worked tirelessly to secure grants and donations for the professorship. A note scribbled by Monahan laid out the scope of the fundraising campaign. It showed two hoped for areas of support; the first listed $200,000 from the B.C. government and B.C. businesses, and the second showed $200,000 from corporations within and outside Washington.[5] Monahan, assisted by Jeanene DeLille, executive director of the University Foundation, prepared an extensive list of entities and individuals to be approached for contributions to the professorship. Just a partial listing gives an idea of the scope of the campaign: CanFor Corporation in Vancouver; Devonian Foundation in Calgary; Canadian Pacific Foundation; Government of British Columbia; The Weyerhaeuser Corporation; Business Fund for Canadian Studies in the United States; Chevron; Burlington Northern; the Donner Foundation in New York. None of these requests yielded hard cash, with typical reasons being: "we don't fund endowments"; "funding of this kind is only to honor our own retired leaders"; "we only fund Canadian universities"; "funds are in short supply." Fortunately, the Western Foundation promised to underwrite the needed $150,000, a necessary action to ensure the state matching money would not be lost.

A devastating tragedy loomed that would alter the contours of Western's leadership ranks and change the funding terms of the professorship. On November 4, 1987, President Ross along with Western vice presidents Jeanene DeLille and Donald Cole, attended a university fundraising event in Tacoma, Washington, about 120 miles south of Bellingham. Later that evening, the three of them boarded a small chartered Cessna for the flight back home. On approaching the Bellingham airport, something went terribly wrong and the plane crashed in forested land about ten miles north of the airport. Ross, DeLille and Cole were killed along with the pilot, Ty Hardan. The crushing tragedy severely shocked the university. The human loss was heartbreaking and the cost of losing three top school officials was immeasurable. In Olympia, the state capital, the tragedy was deeply felt as Ross was well-liked by legislators and known as one of the state's most effective college presidents. The governor ordered state flags to be flown at half-mast and the massive outpouring of condolences from Olympia reinforced the magnitude of the loss.

As a way of commemorating the president, the state legislature decided to make a special appropriation of $500,000 to create the G. Robert Ross Distinguished Professorship Award. The terms of the grant were unchanged from those of the special professorship awarded before the plane tragedy. The full name was the G. Robert Ross Distinguished Professorship of Canada–U.S. Business and Economic Relations. With the addition of the already committed $100,000 from the Government of Canada, the total endowment for the professorship was now $600,000. The university provided a permanent faculty position at the level of full professor. In accordance with the state guidelines for the professorship, endowment earning would be used to fund staff support, research costs and public outreach events in business and government circles conducted by the professor. The original idea of a "rotating" visiting professorship, where individuals would come for short terms, was retained.

Alan Rugman a distinguished economist from the University of Toronto, was selected to be the first Ross professor. His inauguration was a major Bellingham event headlined by a large and elegant dinner at the Leopold Hotel, hosted by Western's president and attended by a spectrum of academic and civic leaders. In wide ranging remarks, he recommended that the three North American Nations (U.S., Canada and Mexico) form a European type of common market, portending the NAFTA agreement signed four years later. He viewed the Pacific Northwest, British Columbia and Japan as an up and coming trading block and predicted closer ties among their economies would bring significant benefits to Washington and British Columbia. A specialist in international business and an advisor to two Canadian prime ministers, Rugman taught courses, conducted research and organized conferences that brought top economists and business leaders from across North America to Western. The endowed professorship was not conceived as a research-centered position and Rugman set the standard for the Ross professors who followed him by working closely with business and political leaders from Vancouver to Seattle, as well as with academics from across North America, to make the professorship not only a major teaching resource, but just as importantly a vital force for public education on Canadian business and trade matters.

The Ross professorship, coupled with the economics position leveraged from Title VI funding, formed the nucleus of Canadian economic expertise that considerably enriched the Canadian–American Studies undergraduate curriculum and the MBA program in the College of Business and Economics. The Center had successfully secured federal and state money to augment its relatively lean university resources to add faculty in a key area in its quest to bolster Canadian–American Studies and attain national recognition.

7
The Culture Turn

A Second Distinguished Professorship

By the end of the 1980s, Canadian–American Studies at Western had reached a new plateau. The first endowed professorship at the university was established, dedicated to Canadian–U.S. business and economic relations, with its first occupant the distinguished University of Toronto economist, Alan Rugman. The curriculum dealing with the Canadian economy was further bolstered by the appointment of a new tenure-track faculty member, Mary-Ann Hendryson, an economist who was completing her Ph.D. studies at Washington State University. In the history department, Elizabeth Mancke was hired to a tenure-track position to replace retiring Harley Hiller. Other faculty positions in French and environmental studies were near approval. The number of students annually taking Canadian–American Studies courses that were part of the major or minor numbered over 1,200. The introductory CanAm 200 class had reached an enrollment high of 220 students in 1990. The Center's outreach programs were flourishing. Indeed, a 1989 External Evaluation report stated that Western had "the best Canadian Studies outreach program in the West, exemplified by the Royal Roads, Edmonton, Study Canada and French language workshops and by quality publications."[1] The Center continued to be guided very skillfully by the entrepreneurial Bob Monahan with support from new university president

Kenneth Mortimer.

What was missing, or at least underdeveloped in the program, was the broad area of culture, and particularly the subjects of Canadian Francophone language, Indigenous peoples, multiculturalism and literature. French language was of course an integral part of the Foreign Language program. However, except for a summer workshop on French Canadian Culture and Literature, there was no focus on the culture of Francophone societies in Canada. Similarly, study of Canadian Indigenous peoples was not developed. A sturdy foundation existed in the anthropology department where two faculty, Dan Boxberger and Sara Campbell, taught courses and conducted research on Native Peoples of the Northwest. Following Ken Innis' retirement in 1992, Canadian literature was no longer a regular offering in the English department. Clearly some building blocks were in place to advance work in Canadian culture but much more was needed.

Planning for strengthening cultural components of Canadian Studies began in the late-1980s. The centerpiece of this effort was a second endowed professorship—a Canadian Culture Distinguished Professorship—to be modeled on the recently created Ross position. The concept of a culture professorship was exciting because it was unique in the United States and it would be an important force for diversifying the program. A prominent position in Canadian culture would fit with the university's push to internationalize the curriculum by strengthening international studies and study abroad programs and diversifying the faculty. Monahan, in advocating for the culture professorship, pointed out that the "presence of Distinguished Professors in the various humanities departments would benefit the university as a whole," and not just Canadian–American Studies. "They would," he continued, "provide an ongoing stimulus to the faculty, our students and our community in perpetuity. This makes the whole idea of a Distinguished Professorship of Canadian Culture a very exciting concept."[2]

A question that was asked was why a dedicated professorship in Canadian culture? Could the university really afford to invest in an area that, although inventive, was highly general and not tied to a traditional discipline? For most Americans, the concept of Canadian culture was esoteric at best. Canadian culture was central to Canadian Studies in Canada, but even there few if any endowed professorships in Canadian culture existed. So, what made Monahan and his colleagues think this idea could work at Western? One reason was because culture crossed virtually all the disciplines in the humanities and most aspects of social science, the position could be used to enhance many programs. This kind of flexibility appealed to administrators faced with tight budgets. A second point was that a professorship in Canadian culture would be distinctive, attract attention and help to differentiate Canadian–American Studies at Western from similar programs elsewhere. This could be helpful in attracting new resources. Another reason was that Canada was becoming recognized globally as a model of a successful multicultural—and multinational—society with many different voices and forms of cultural expression. For academics outside of Canadian Studies, knowledge of Canadian society was timely and valuable for comparative and global studies of effective pluralistic societies. A practical consideration was also on the mind of the Center director. The culture position, unlike the Ross professorship, would be located in Canadian–American Studies and not a department or college where chairs and deans may wish to alter the focus of the position.

The strategy for procuring the culture professorship for Western was similar to that of the Ross position. The university would apply for $250,000 to be made available through the state's distinguished professor program. The Canadian government and other potential donors would be approached for the remaining $250,000 as matching dollars to secure the state funds.

Finding donors for such an unconventional professorship proved to be challenging. Monahan with help and encouragement from the Canadian Consul in Seattle, Dick Seaborn, approached the Canadian government and secured a commitment of $100,000 on the condition that it would be used to leverage other monies. A proposal requesting $208,000 submitted to the National

Endowment for the Humanities was not funded, despite Monahan's personal meetings with NEH officials in Washington, D.C., and a re-submission of the grant proposal at their request. The Donner Foundation in New York was also approached for $250,000 but declined. Several individuals—many of them Western alumni who lived in Canada—were asked to make a significant contribution in return for naming the professorship. A few expressed interest, but none would make the move. So, to avoid losing the initial commitment from the state's distinguished professor program, the Western Foundation underwrote the $150,000 needed to obtain the state money with the expectation that private monies would be eventually raised to cover the investment.

The new professorship, finalized in 1994, was based in Canadian–American Studies, though the holder of the position would be affiliated with a department that fit the individual's field of expertise. Like with the Ross professorship, the university was expected to provide salary support at the full professor level. Departments in the arts and humanities could nominate people in advance, with the possibility that prospective candidates for the position could be preapproved for future years. This kind of planning, it was thought, would ease the problems of finding housing in Bellingham and arranging leaves at the person's home university or other place of work. Following the Ross model, holders of the professorship would serve for short terms, normally two to three years, thereby ensuring that different expertise would regularly cycle through the university's arts and humanities departments.

In 1996, Dr. Valerie Alia, a faculty member at the University of Western Ontario School of Journalism, was appointed Western's first Distinguished Professor of Canadian Culture. Alia had an eclectic and interdisciplinary background. A dual citizen of Canada and the United States, her career spanned work as an art critic, photographer and documentary filmmaker, much of it dealing with Indigenous peoples in the Canadian North. After a career in journalism, she earned her doctorate in Social and Political Thought from York University in Toronto. Between teaching positions at several universities, she traveled extensively in the Canadian North working as a consultant, artist and documentary writer for CBC and other media networks. While at Western, Alia's courses and research dealt with First Nations media, intercultural communication and journalism ethics.

The official dedication of the professorship was held on October 16, 1996, to coincide with the beginning of Alia's term at Western. The well-attended event was headlined by First Nations playwright and performer Margo Kane, recognized internationally for her contributions to the advancement of Indigenous theater. One month later, on November 17, the dedication continued with a performance by the renowned Canadian vocalist and pianist Diana Krall in front of an overflow crowd in the university's concert hall. Not present in person, but certainly in spirit, was former Canadian Consul Dick Seaborn, who had been highly instrumental in lining up Canadian government support for the culture professorship. Excited that Western had established a second endowed chair in Canadian–American Studies, Seaborn penned a note of congratulations to Monahan saying, "You had the idea, then plans, then the selling job, etc. I recall clearly the gleam in your eye and your enthusiasm when you first raised with me the question of a Distinguished Professorship of Canadian Culture at Western Washington University. I was pleased to be able to help. I am positively delighted that it is now a reality." Knowing the difficulty of selling the idea of Canadian culture in a U.S. university, in no little part because of increased pressure on the liberal arts from the sciences, technology and business, Seaborn concluded his note with this comment: "The Philistines have been beaten back for once. Long may you keep them on the run!"[3]

Alia's two-year term was followed by the appointment of Gary Geddes, an award-winning poet and novelist from British Columbia, for the period 1998–2001. Geddes was one of Canada's finest writers of narrative poetry and was a bundle of energy who seemed to know personally every writer in Canada. Possessing a delightful wit, he referred to his tenure at Western as "Operation Trojan Horse: Notes on the Canadian Takeover of the United States." Indeed, he led a cross-border invasion of sorts by bringing more than forty Canadian writers/artists to campus during his three-year term. The list included luminaries in Canadian culture such as Haida artist/mythologist Bill Reid, poet Robert Kroetch, aboriginal playwright Thomson Highway, Cree poet Louise Halfe, poet/historian George Bowering, poet/linguist, Robert Bringhurst, and novelist Daphne Marlatt, to name only a few. Geddes was affiliated with the English department and taught classes on Canadian fiction, poetry, and creative writing. Living on a sailboat in the Bellingham Bay harbor, Geddes held his classes in Canada House during dinner time with the requirement that the students in the class trade off doing the cooking.

Western's library's holdings on Canadian literature were modest at best. To help remedy the situation, Geddes took it upon himself to write letters to more than 200 Canadian writers and publishers across the country asking them to donate their works to Western's library. It was an extraordinarily generous act that resulted in the university receiving more than 700 books! The library with support from the university administration arranged a formal dedication ceremony to thank Geddes and especially the Canadian writers and publishers, several of whom were present at the event. The plan for the ceremony was to have a large contingent of Canadian and U.S. dignitaries and college officials speak. Geddes politely objected, saying that he did not want the writers and publishers "overshadowed by the bureaucrats." "Let's keep the focus on the tribute to the writers," he wrote in a memo to the organizers. "After all, bureaucrats are giving away public funds; writers and publishers are giving away their own."[4]

Bringing outstanding Canadian writers, artists and performers to campus was a hallmark of the Canadian culture professorship. The appointment of Lee Maracle to be the third holder of the position in 2001 continued the trend. Maracle, a member of the Squamish Nation located north of Vancouver, B.C., and one of Canada's foremost writers and orators on Aboriginal and feminist issues, offered a unique perspective on the interaction between Canadian and First Nations cultures. She founded the En'owkin International School of Writing in B.C. and held several university positions, including the Stanley Knowles Visiting Professorship in Canadian Studies at the University of Waterloo and a writing professorship at the University of Toronto. Her work includes poetry, short stories, performances and several books, the most widely known are *Ravensong, I am Woman, Sojourner's Truth, Bobbi Lee, Indian Rebel* and *Daughters are Forever.* While at Western, Maracle taught courses on modern Native literature and creative writing, conducted several Indigenous writers' workshops and did a number of performance readings for audiences on and off campus.

The success of the culture professorship in fostering awareness of Canada's cultural landscape and enriching artistic activities on the university campus and in the community is unquestioned. The sheer number of visiting artists, writers and historians touched virtually every department and program in the arts and humanities and spilled over into some areas of social sciences. Students were the main beneficiaries as the professorship put them in the presence—always in small, intimate classes—of a continuous stream of world class talent.

Unfortunately, the position's inadequate funding structure undermined its long-term viability. When recruitment for the position began in 1995, Provost DeLorme declared that only 50 percent of the professorship salary would be paid from the university budget, meaning that the other 50 percent would have to come from the endowment earnings fund. DeLorme gave no reason for departing from what had been the understanding of Canadian–American Studies that a full FTE would be allotted to the position—following the model of the Ross professorship. DeLorme's decision to halve the university's share of the salary made it unfeasible to continue hiring prominent individuals for the position. By the end of 2002, the earnings fund was nearly depleted which meant, barring an infusion of new money from outside the university, the budget for the professorship was no longer solvent enough to fund a full-time visiting faculty. The professorship was transformed into a funding stream for speakers, short-term visiting scholars and special culture performances—clearly not what was intended when the endowment was created. In 2010, when the university faced its largest budget cuts since the 1970s, the university funded portion of the salary for this innovative position was taken away and never reinstated.

Francophone Language and Literature

Western's French program, like most in the United States, was oriented toward Parisian French. Although some French professors touched on the Francophone reality in Canada, there was no commitment by anyone in the foreign languages department to this important part of Canadian Studies. To remedy this problem, funds for hiring a French professor with expertise on Québec were written in to a Title VI grant in the early 1990s. Following the model used in economics, 50 percent of this new position was paid for by the U.S. Department of Education for a three-year period, to be followed by full university funding thereafter. The occupant of the tenure-track position would be based in the French program with significant responsibilities in Canadian–American Studies.

In 1992, Dr. Louise-Marie Bouchard was appointed to the new position. Bouchard, a native of Québec with degrees from McGill University, the University of Montreal and the University of Sherbrooke, designed a core course on Québec language and culture (Civilisation et Culture de Québec) and also taught a more general course emphasizing the distinctive characteristics of French language in Québec. Bouchard organized study opportunities for Western students in Québec through the University of Laval Intensive French Language Program in Québec City. Her courses were popular and she quickly attracted a solid student following.

Bouchard's appointment and the French program's growing interest in Québec caught the attention of the Québec Government Office in Los Angeles, which was attempting to promote economic and cultural knowledge of Canada's French-speaking province in American universities. Recognizing that Western Washington University was one of the few American institutions in the western part of the country where anything on Québec was being taught, the Québec Government Office looked favorably on the Canadian–American Studies program. It provided speakers, financial support for student and faculty exchanges, and grants to help strengthen library and media resources in Québec studies.

During this time, French Professor Robert Balas, aided by another French program faculty member, Anne George, developed an interest in Québec film and began building a large collection of Québec video. Balas, a talented cartoonist who taught conversational French by utilizing computers to animate his drawings of French-speaking Québeckers, conducted several five-day summer seminars for high school teachers titled "Atelier de Francais." Each was innovative, using technology to teach French, incorporating Québecois theater, French language radio, video and film, and arranging visiting presentations from Québecois artists and professors. Eventually the teaching of French language and film in Québec evolved into one of the strongest elements of the Center's curriculum and educational outreach. This was noticed in an outside evaluation of the Center conducted in 1996, where one evaluator concluded: "I believe that the French program represents a major strength for the Canadian Studies program."[5]

Leadership Changes: The Early 1990s

In 1992, Bob Monahan announced he would be stepping down as director and retiring at the end of the calendar year. For the first time since 1976 the directorship would change. Monahan called a meeting of Canadian–American Studies affiliated faculty (referred to at the time as The Canadian Studies Advisory Committee) to discuss options and ultimately settle on a candidate whose name would then be forwarded to the provost for official action. I served as the unofficial associate director (the position had never been formalized by the university administration) and had worked with Bob from almost the time he took over the program in 1976. Because we had worked so closely together for so long, it must have seemed obvious to him and presumably other faculty members that I would be the natural successor. A vote was held and I being the sole candidate nominated was elected. The vote of the faculty was a recommendation to the provost, although faculty recommendations on chairs and directors—notwithstanding the Manfred Vernon controversy—normally were given considerable weight.

When reviewing archival documents for this book, I learned that what seemed at the time to be a straightforward noncontroversial process was anything but. When Monahan notified Provost DeLorme that I had been elected by a unanimous vote of the Canadian Studies Advisory Committee on May 19, 1992, DeLorme wrote back:

> Bob, you know that I cannot allow program directors to be selected in this manner. In "reminding" me of past history, you [Monahan] neglected to note that, before you were selected, the [Canadian Studies] group had unanimously elected Manfred Vernon, and that selection was rejected by the President. I expect you to handle this matter, so that I do not have to embarrass Alper.[6]

DeLorme then requested that Monahan form a search committee from the full complement of Canadian–American Studies faculty, to conduct a campus-wide search for a director to take office in fall 1993. In the meantime, DeLorme said he would choose an acting director to fill in from January through August 1993.

As far as I know, no search was held, nor do I recall having any knowledge that a search was even contemplated, or why DeLorme had a problem with the action taken by the Canadian Studies Advisory Committee. As it turned out I was offered the position of acting director with no specific term of office and no explanation of what DeLorme had in mind for the long term. I assumed his action was to allow some period of time to pass before converting the position from "acting" to director. Perhaps this was his way of making the entire process seem more deliberative. As for the campus-wide search, I do not know if it ever occurred.

Would I take the position? I was of two minds about succeeding Bob as director of the Center. Having worked closely with him for the past 16 years, I felt prepared and believed I could make a contribution. At the same time, I realized the position required a strong commitment to administrative work which would likely overshadow teaching and research. Was this what I wanted as I entered my 22nd year at Western? In the end, I decided to take the position but only if staff resources were increased and the position had sufficient release time from teaching. Bob continued to do great things with far too little release from his faculty duties, and without enough secretarial help. As every outside evaluation of the Center repeatedly said, directors were expected to do too much with too little. My conditions for taking the directorship, communicated to the chair of my department (political science) and the provost were: 1) a dedicated full time secretarial/program manager; and, 2) 50 percent release time from teaching in the political science department. The secretarial request was granted, but the provost balked on the request for more release time. A compromise was struck where the requested 50 per cent release would be divided between political science (25 percent) and the provost's office (25 percent). I found it objectionable that political science should have to fund part of the Canadian Studies director position. However, the chair of political science, Kenneth Hoover, initiated and supported the idea, probably assuming that the release time charged to the department would be assumed by the provost's budget sooner rather than later. I also believe Hoover saw advantages for the political science department in having one of its faculty direct a growing interdisciplinary program with steady federal funding from both the Canadian and U.S. governments.

I was appointed acting director in late 1992 and began my duties on January 1, 1993. It should be noted that it was not until 1999 that the half time position was funded in full by the provost's budget. Until that time, the political science department paid for 25 percent of the Canadian–American Studies' director position, receiving in return funds to pay for temporary nontenured faculty to teach in my stead. As for the change in my "acting" status, I don't know when my position formally changed to director; it just happened.

I would be remiss if I did not discuss a vital part of the Center's new leadership structure; new program manager, Martha (Marty)

Hitchcock. Almost immediately following my appointment, I began the hiring process for a full-time program manager. The growing program needed a steady hand who could help manage the external activities conducted frequently by the Center and, most important, keep track of the financial details of a budget comprised of numerous grants and other funding sources. The largest source of funding was the Title VI federal grant. We always had three or four annual grants from the Canadian government to help fund the Study Canada program, various new program initiatives, conferences and assorted faculty research projects. In addition, there were various grants from other entities. Keeping track of these different funds which normally rolled over from year to year was not onerous but it required fighting off the administrators in the grants' office who were set on consolidating the many small grants into one. Our Title VI grant shared with the University of Washington was a sinkhole of bureaucratic routine, the management of which I was only too happy to delegate to the program manager. I still remember Marty's response during her job interview to my question about how she felt about extensive budget responsibilities should she get the position: "I love numbers and I love working with budgets!" I don't think much else was said as I knew then she was the right person. I was certainly proved right. Marty not only kept the books flawlessly, but provided a level of organization and efficiency to the program that were the envy of colleagues across the university. Beyond this, her dedication and ebullient personality made her a perfect ambassador for the Center and all things Canadian on the campus and to myriad business, government and NGO constituencies we dealt with.

In 1993, the presidency of Western Washington University changed with the appointment of Dr. Karen Morse to replace Kenneth Mortimer, who was leaving Western to become president and chancellor of the University of Hawai'i system. Morse, a professor of chemistry who held numerous patents and awards, had been the provost at Utah State University before coming to Western. Among her distinctions was winning the Olin-Garvin Medal, the highest award given to a woman for her contributions to chemistry. The first female president of Western, Morse greatly strengthened the university's science programs. As for Canada, her familiarity with the country didn't go much beyond her visits to Canada while growing up in Monroe, Michigan, a small town one hour south of Windsor, Ontario. However, she quickly realized the academic value of the program and especially the potential research and public policy activities that could assist the state and national policy communities. Morse became in my judgment the strongest presidential advocate for the Center in its history and played a pivotal role in the creation of the Border Policy Research Institute in 2005.

A goal of the Center for many years was to strengthen teaching and research on Canadian environmental policy in Huxley College of the Environment. Progress in achieving this goal was slow because Huxley's deans and chairs had not paid a great deal of attention to Canada, despite ongoing dynamic and highly publicized cross-border environmental issues affecting Washington state, Canada and other parts of the Pacific Northwest region. Individual faculty had connections with Canada, particularly John Miles, a Huxley professor and former dean of the college and an accomplished author and historian of the North Cascades—the mountain range that straddles the Canadian border and extends south to Oregon. Miles' acclaimed work in environmental education inevitably linked him and his students with the Canadian environmental community. But Miles' interest in Canada was mostly peripheral to his work in environmental education.

Another Huxley faculty member with Canadian ties was Bert Webber, a marine biologist with family roots in British Columbia, who approached his teaching and research on Washington and B.C. coastal waters from the perspective of examining one ecosystem, thereby bringing Canadian marine ecology into all aspects of his work. Huxley professor Lynn Robbins included Canadian comparisons in his environmental policy courses. Still, a Canadian Studies foothold in the Huxley faculty and curriculum was missing.

This changed in 1994 when Bradley Smith, formerly the director of Environmental Education at the United States Environmental

Robert Kaiser in 1966.

President Harvey Bunke in 1966.

Dr. Manfred Vernon, right, discusses race relations, the Vietnam War, and American foreign policy with Georgia State Legislator and Civil Rights activist Julian Bond, center, for a KVOS special hosted by Duayne F. Trecker, left, on May 19, 1967.

Courtesy Barry Gough
Professor Barry Gough, circa 1970.

Special Collections WWU
Western President Jerry Flora, left, and symposium coordinator Gerard Rutan flank Washington Gov. Dan Evans, seated, in Olympia announcing the Canadian–American Symposium in 1974.

Special Collections WWU
Canadian–American Studies Director, Gerard Rutan (at podium) introduces, from left, British Columbia Premier Dave Barrett, Western Washington State College President Jerry Flora and Gov. Dan Evans at the Canadian–American Symposium, September 1974.

Special Collections WWU

Canadian Consul General Ian Wood, left, and Western President Paul Olscamp after the presentation of a library grant from the Government of Canada, March, 1978. In backround, from left: Head of Bureau for Faculty Research Jane Clark, Dean James Davis, Sam Kelly, (unidentified person), and Don Alper.

40th Anniversary Presentation Slide

Canada House, circa 1980.

President Paul Olscamp presents Canadian Consul General, J.C. Gordon Brown with a gift during dedication ceremonies at Canada House in February 1979.

Special Collections WWU

Robert Monahan receiving thanks from James Colthart of the Canadian Embassy on the occasion of the dedication of Canada House in February 1979.

Special Collections WWU

Don Alper (center) talking with participants at U.S.-Canada Forestry Institute at Canada House in April 1980.

Special Collections WWU

Left: Campus Planner and State Representative Barney Goltz with Robert Monahan at presentation of Canadian and U.S. flags to be flown from Canada House, February 1980.

Below: Robert Monahan staffing the Canadian–American Studies booth in Red Square during Canada Week May 1980.

Special Collections WWU

Canada House photos

Geographer James Scott, left, discusses archival maps with Canadian Embassy's Academic Relations Officer, Norm London, in the Pacific Northwest Studies Archives in the basement of Canada House, May 1981.

Faculty and staff gather in front of Canada House on the occasion of the grand opening of the Faculty Club on October 1, 1982.

Special Collections WWU
President G. Robert Ross in 1983.

Special Collections WWU
President Karen Morse in 1993.

Special Collections WWU
Acting President Larry DeLorme, right, receiving a check for the Distinguished Professorship of Canadian Culture from Bernard Gagosz, Consul General of Canada, Seattle, April 1993.

Canada House photo
From left: Don Alper, Canadian Ambassador Raymond Chretien, Marty Hitchcock, Consul General Roger Simmons and Bob Monahan, February 16, 2000, at Canada House.

Canada House photo

Associate Professor of French and Linguistics, Dr. Christina Keppie, left, talking with students in 2015. Keppie assumed the directorship of the Center for Canadian–American Studies in 2018, the first woman to hold the post.

Canada House photo

Geography professor Dr. David Rossiter became director of the Center in 2014.

Courtesy L. Trautman

Dr. Laurie Trautman was named Border Policy Research Institute director in 2016.

Canada House photo

David Davidson, then-Associate Director of the BPRI, talks with Canadian Consul Wendy Baldwin (left) and Kathy Reigstad, Managing Editor of ARCS, at a gathering in 2010.

Protection Agency, was selected as the new dean of Huxley College. Smith came to Western with both a personal and professional interest in Canada. A native of Michigan, he spent a good deal of his personal life in Canada. Professionally, he was knowledgeable about Canadian environmental policy having conducted research on waterfowl and wetlands for Environment Canada and the Canadian Fish and Wildlife Service in the Great Lakes Region. He also had served as a member of President Bill Clinton's Council for Sustainable Development where he advised the Council on Educational Strategies, a body that did some work related to cross-border environments. Because Smith was a policy guy with an attachment to Canada, I thought it reasonable to try to persuade him to hire a new faculty member with a focus on Canadian environmental policy.

Much was happening in Canada–U.S. environmental politics both regionally and nationally. Washington state and British Columbia had signed an innovative state/province environmental cooperation agreement in 1992, and at the national level, the two countries were attempting to strengthen cooperation on matters ranging from fisheries to air pollution. Also interest among students and faculty in cross-border wilderness areas and marine sanctuaries in the Salish Sea was growing. A new position devoted to Canadian environmental policy would fortify connections between the Center and Huxley, and it would strengthen Western's role as a player in regional environmental politics. The strategy used was to once again leverage a new position with Title VI grant money.

The opportunity availed itself in 1995 when the Title VI grant was up for renewal. Dean Smith approved a new position in Canadian environmental policy in Huxley College. Like with those in economics, filled by Mary-Ann Hendryson, and in French, by Louise-Marie Bouchard, the grant would fund 50 percent of the Huxley post for the first three years, after which it would be permanently funded by the university. The job description was written broadly to focus on environmental policy and law with an emphasis on Canada.

Jean Melious, who held a Master of Philosophy from the University of Edinburgh in urban design and regional planning and a law degree from Harvard and had practiced law in Canada, was hired in 1996. Melious quickly became involved in cross-border air and water issues and, in addition to attracting students to Canadian Studies, became active in NGOs and consulting work linked to governments in both countries. The door was opened and soon more and more Huxley faculty and students became interested in Canada, often encouraged by grant opportunities made available by the Canadian government and ongoing Title VI grants.

Border Environments North and South

When assuming the directorship of the Center, a goal of mine was to promote more teaching, research and public outreach in the area of transboundary environmental studies. This seemed to be a no-brainer considering our location near the border and the fact that Western was home to one of the nation's premier environmental colleges. The Center's 1993 academic plan made this point:

> The Canadian Studies program is well positioned to take advantage of the increasing interest in environmental issues as it relates to transborder environmental problems and policy questions. We are uniquely situated by geography and academically well qualified with Huxley College of Environmental Studies to capitalize in this area.[7]

The passage of the North American Free Trade Agreement (NAFTA) in 1994 brought fresh attention to the U.S.–Mexico borderlands and sparked interest in incorporating a trilateral dimension into the Center's programs. The Earth Summit, held in Rio de Janeiro, Brazil, in 1992, was a turning point in raising consciousness about the importance of working across national boundaries to achieve what was then being called sustainable development. Border regions, where the effects of economic development and urban growth were considerable—with both positive and negative impacts—were seen as laboratories for the application of sustainability practices.

A noteworthy transboundary conference dealing with sustainable development in the Cascadia Corridor stretching from British

Columbia to Oregon was organized by the Center in 1993. The idea for the conference came from discussions with Bruce Agnew, a former Snohomish, Washington, county councilman and congressional staffer, and John Miller, a former Seattle congressman. Agnew was the founder of the Cascadia Center of the Discovery Institute, a regionalist organization in Seattle aimed at getting British Columbia, Washington, and Oregon to work in common in such areas as rail transportation, trade, tourism, environmental protection and technology. After a campus visit by Agnew and Miller in early 1993, it was decided to hold a large international meeting at Western in September at which leaders and citizens of Washington, Oregon and British Columbia would share ideas about sustainable development and devise strategies for common action, including a role for the region's universities. The title of the ambitious conference, "Georgia Basin, Puget Sound, Willamette Valley International Conference: Building Bridges to Sustainable Communities," set out the British Columbia to Oregon geographical scope it would cover.

I viewed the conference as an opportunity to position the university—and the Center—as a leader in efforts to enhance cooperation with B.C. in key economic sectors and work side by side with the province to protect the shared environment. The premier of British Columbia and the governors of Oregon and Washington endorsed the conference, adding to its importance. The Center took the lead in organizing the event, with the Seattle-based Cascadia Center, and particularly Bruce Agnew, providing vital assistance by drawing on their metropolitan connections to help raise funds and recruit key business and environmental leaders, especially in Washington and Oregon.

Obtaining the necessary funding for what was turning into a large and complicated conference proved to be an ordeal in itself. Initial base funding was provided by Western ($5,000) and a grant from the Canadian Embassy ($7,000). The funding plan was to target large companies such as Microsoft, and local, state and provincial government agencies throughout the Cascadia Corridor region. Agnew had good contacts in the Seattle area and was confident that he and his colleagues could raise the lion's share of the money needed. Agnew's organization provided $5,000 to add to the base funding and promised more as the outcomes of their fundraising campaign allowed. Agnew was successful in getting contributions from Battelle Pacific Laboratories, the Henry M. Jackson Foundation, and the Northwest Electric Power and Planning Council. Additional grants came from SeaFirst Bank and Bellingham-based Brown and Cole Stores, Inc.

This was not enough, however, as the funds raised in grants and donations amounted to about half of what was budgeted to conduct the conference. A significant budget shortfall could have ended the event, but Western's organizers believed there was too much at stake for the Center and the university for the conference to fail. Fundraising efforts continued although time was running out. The Western Foundation, already invested in the project, agreed to underwrite the deficit, based on a promise by the organizers that dollars would be forthcoming at some point to cover the commitment. In the last two weeks preceding the event the conference team embarked on a large-scale phone and fax campaign to drive up conference registrations, which were moneymakers. The result was the number of paid registrations skyrocketed. The success of this campaign was due to unending hours put in by conference staffers Rob Kelly and Robyn DuPre, and several volunteers who worked right up to the day the conference began. Kelly, a Western political science graduate student and the principal conference staff person, was paid a minimal salary, scrounged from various parts of the Center's budget. DuPre, also a graduate student, worked as a volunteer. Numerous other volunteers—mostly students, old and young—were signed up to help with endless conference details, including 13-year-old Elyse Alper who helped with mailings and other paperwork. The hard work paid off as costs were covered and the conference turned out to be a high-profile event for the Center.

The conference had several "firsts." It was the first cross-border regional gathering in the Pacific Northwest that attempted to address sustainability in an integrated way. Sixty-six speakers and more than 300 participants (including many high school and college students) discussed environmental cooperation, social equity issues, sustainable economies, transportation challenges, farmland preservation, property rights, regional energy issues and cross-border data-sharing. These deliberations led to several recommendations, perhaps the most important being the creation of a regional network for information sharing to help make the Oregon–Washington–British Columbia transnational region a model of sustainability. Another first was bringing agency and departmental officials together from the three state and provincial jurisdictions to meet and deliberate on common issues. For most of them, this was the first time they had ever met and talked with a counterpart from the other state and province.

On campus, the conference strengthened the Center's ties with Huxley College and the International Studies program. Collaborative efforts with these programs would be more common in the future, and more students and faculty in the rapidly growing field of environmental studies would look to the Canada–U.S. shared environment as an important study area.

The conference set the stage for future work, and during the next few years, several cross-border environmental workshops and conferences were undertaken by the Center. To get a sense of the range of these activities, it is worth mentioning at least the main ones: In the summer of 1994, a two-week international environmental workshop for science teachers was held in the upper Skagit River Valley of the North Cascades Range which spans the Canada–U.S. border. In 1996, the Center hosted "Salmon Know No Borders," a one-week environmental education workshop for K–12 teachers. In summer 1997, a follow-up five-day environmental education workshop for teachers was held titled "Salmon Know No Borders: Canada–U.S. Policy Issues." In May 1998, a two-day conference titled "Shared Waters/Shared Stewardship," addressed environmental problems stemming from growth and development in Washington's Puget Sound and British Columbia's Georgia Basin marine areas (now called the Salish Sea). In summer 1999, a third environmental education workshop was held titled, "Who Owns the Sea? Exploring Whale and Salmon Issues Across the Canada–U.S. Border."

The Culture Turn

During this period, Western was the site for several environmental meetings sponsored by government agencies in British Columbia and Washington. In 1995, Western hosted the annual meeting of the B.C.–Washington Environmental Cooperation Council. This group, created by the B.C.–Washington Environmental Agreement, enacted in 1992, served as a forum for the state and province to work in common on environmental problems with cross-border impacts. The council provided a framework for state and provincial officials to work cooperatively to monitor and mitigate air pollution, alleviate contaminants in cross-border rivers and streams, protect ground water that percolates across the border and lessen toxics and other human-made stressors that adversely affect the health of the Salish Sea. Between 1997 and 2001, Canada House hosted four workshops comprising government officials and environmental NGO leaders from each side of the border. The meetings, led by officials from Environment Canada and the U.S. Environmental Protection Agency (EPA) regional offices, produced action plans for aligning transboundary airshed policies and "smart growth" strategies undertaken by the state and province. Canada House had become a highly desirable site for conducting state/provincial conferences and policy workshops because of Western's location, confidence in the Center's work and the fact that faculty and graduate students were able to participate in these events, adding local expertise and providing students "hands on" knowledge of important aspects of Canada–U.S. relations.

Also in the 1990s, the Center leveraged grant monies to add novel courses dealing with transborder sustainability and other environmental topics. In 1997 political science professor Debra Salazar and I developed a course on sustainability of forests across the Washington–B.C. region. The course featured alternating Canadian and American speakers and became the basis for a book published by UBC Press titled, *Sustaining the Forests of the Pacific Coast*. In 1998, geography professor Patrick Buckley joined with colleague John Belec at the University of the Fraser Valley in Abbotsford, British Columbia, to offer a joint course on environmental planning in the Fraser Lowland region which encompasses the Fraser Valley on the Canadian side of the border and Whatcom County on the American side. Students worked in cross-border research teams and classes were held on both sides of the border. At the time, the course was the only undergraduate course of its kind anywhere along the span of the Canada–U.S. border. Another cross-border course—offered in 2001 and 2002—linked students and faculty at the University of British Columbia, Western, and the University of Washington. The course titled "Managing an International Ecosystem" examined environmental problems facing the Puget Sound and Georgia Basin region and cross-border solutions—highlighting different Canadian and American perspectives on policy prescriptions. Students from the three universities were joined by faculty from the Sustainable Development Research Institute at UBC, the Center for Canadian–American Studies at WWU, the Battelle Research Center (Seattle) and School of Environmental Studies at UW. The 1990s and early 2000s were a time of considerable expansion of environmental studies into subject areas related to the Canada–U.S. border.

New interest in comparative North American (Canada–U.S.–Mexico) borders was also having an impact on Canadian Studies. As noted above, the passage of the North American Free Trade Agreement brought more political attention to the southern border and stirred a debate within the Canadian Studies community over how traditional Canada–U.S. Studies fit with emerging North American relationships involving Canada, the U.S. and Mexico. Some academics were arguing that Canadian Studies in the U.S. should be amalgamated within a broader North American Studies orientation, with a dual focus on Canada and Mexico This was what happened at Duke University. Duke's long-standing Canadian Studies program was merged with a sister program dealing with Mexican and Latin American Studies. At Western, the discussion centered on how comparative study of America's northern and southern borders and trilateral exchanges involving the United States, Mexico, and Canada could actually strengthen Canadian–American Studies. An important part of this discussion was how to leverage the university's strength in the "niche area of environmental studies" and apply it to both the southern and northern borders.[8]

Interest in expanding the Center's focus from the Canadian border to broader NAFTA border topics was spurred in other ways as well. The Ross professorship sponsored a succession of visiting speakers who weighed NAFTA's impacts; North American free trade inspired a staple of coursework and research in the College of Business and Economics, and the Center and the University of Washington's Jackson School offered two jointly taught courses on NAFTA in 1998 and 1999.

In 1995, the Center in partnership with the Center for International Studies organized the university's first symposium focused on the U.S.–Canada and U.S.–Mexico borders. Titled "Border Demographics and Regional Interdependency: A Trilateral Symposium, Canada/U.S./Mexico," the meeting's purpose was twofold: first to bring together faculty and university leaders from the three countries to examine environmental, infrastructure, economic development and immigration/migration challenges in North American border regions; and second, to map out trilateral educational exchanges and partnerships. The latter purpose was the topic of a keynote roundtable featuring Western President Karen Morse and university leaders from Simon Fraser University, the University of Northern British Columbia, Capilano College in Vancouver, B.C., and El Colegio de La Frontera Norte (COLEF) in Tijuana, Mexico. The conference was successful in creating a foundation for working in common on exchange opportunities along with promoting trilateral teaching and research.

Anthropology Professor James Loucky, a specialist in Latin America and international migration, and the Interim Director of Western's Center for International Studies, was a strong proponent of developing ties with Mexican universities to foster student exchanges. To make this happen, Loucky was successful in getting a $106,000 United States Information Agency planning grant. This was joined with other funding from a Canadian Studies Program Enhancement grant ($6,000) and Fulbright Canada ($4,500). With support from Vice Provost Larry Estrada, a university partnership was formed with Simon Fraser University and COLEF to begin trilateral student exchanges focused on comparative border studies in the U.S.–Mexico and the U.S.–Canada borderlands. Environmental problems in each borderland were the topics of study. Students would spend a quarter or semester each in the B.C.-Washington and California-Mexico borderlands conducting research projects. With on-site observation of water contamination, air quality impacts and other public health problems chronic to border regions, students would get an unusual experiential education, made all the more valuable because of the U.S.-Canada and U.S.-Mexico borderlands comparisons. Professor J. Chadwick Day, Director of the School of Resources and the Environment at Simon Fraser University was the Canadian partner. At El Colegio de la Frontera Norte, Vice President Jorge Santibanez was the lead person. Western, Simon Fraser University and El Colegio de la Frontera Norte signed a formal trilateral agreement forming the consortium, that took place in the presence of Mexican President Ernesto Zedillo in Vancouver at the Pan Pacific Hotel during his state visit to Canada on November 24, 1997.

Recruitment of students for the new border exchange program proved to be more difficult than anticipated. The main problem was lack of travel funds for students. Grant funds generally could not be used to cover costs of student travel—seemingly inexplicable since an overriding purpose of university partnerships is to exchange students. Without adequate support for travel, few if any Mexican students could afford to come to the U.S. or Canada. The American and Canadian students who enrolled in the program were mostly, if not entirely, self-supporting. Efforts were made to get foundation and business support. Several U.S. companies expressed interest but none committed funds. Foundations that supported student travel such as Fulbright and the U.S.-Mexico Foundation declined to provide funding because, as they told us, the design of the exchange program did not fit with the traditional model of university campus-to-university campus international partnerships. Our inability to find outside money to sustain what we thought to be an exciting and innovative program was, needless to say, disappointing.

The three-university consortium, however, proved to be valuable in other ways. In 2001, the Center teamed with SFU and COLEF to organize a conference examining environmental, economic and migration challenges in the Pacific corridor region extending from British Columbia to Baja, California. The goal was to muster a team of academics from the three countries to share research findings, teaching ideas, and exchange opportunities. The research papers were later published as a book (*Transboundary Policy Challenges in the Pacific Border Regions of North America*).

The conference was held over four days at three locations—Bellingham, Vancouver, and Whistler, B.C.—October 25-28, 2001, six weeks after the 9/11 terrorist attacks in New York, Washington, D.C., and Pennsylvania. Although most of the conference planning was completed before 9/11, the program agenda was revised to reflect the changed status of borders in North America. The conference keynote address, titled "North America's Borders After September 11," was given by Jorge Bustamante, president of COLEF and an acclaimed international expert on global migration. In his remarks, Bustamante spoke to how the war on terrorism declared by President George W. Bush had changed both borders making traditional cross-border economic and especially cultural interaction problematic in the future. Bustamante offered a gloomy assessment of life along the U.S.–Mexico border which, in his view, would bear no resemblance to normality as long as the war conditions prevailed. At the conference, some of our Mexican colleagues were affected by the new border reality when they were denied admission into Canada and back into the U.S. because of what they were told was insufficient documentation.

In the years following 9/11, greater restrictions at the border with Mexico sapped interest in the Center's efforts to expand its North American activities. The idea of a more culturally integrated North America in many respects died with America's new obsession with terrorism. The trilateral student border exchange program, already stalled because of lack of funding for student travel, became inactive as the United States, shocked by the 9/11 attacks, became more insular and nationalistic.

A National Profile for Teacher Outreach

By the end of the 1990s the Study Canada teachers' outreach program, a core part of Title VI funding, needed greater institutionalization within the Center. The budget had grown, local and national events increased, and the scope of the curriculum was expanded. The program would now need a staff coordinator and a more established presence in Canada House.

Utilizing Title VI federal funds, a half-time Outreach Coordinator position was created in 2000. The Center was fortunate that a highly capable former teacher with professional experience in both the U.S. and Canada got the job. Tina Storer was an ideal fit for the position. A native of Toronto, she moved to Michigan where she attended the University of Michigan, then transferred to the University of Toronto where she received her B.A. degree. She taught English in Ontario and Québec and spent several years in Montreal (with her husband, WWU economics professor, Paul Storer). Adding to her education credentials and experience in Canada was her passion for educating Americans about Canada. She quickly took the reins of the program and built what came to be widely recognized as the best Canadian Studies teacher outreach program in the nation. During a visit to a Study Canada Summer Institute in Bellingham in 2002, popular CBC Radio producer and columnist Peter Black said:

> The program offered by the Canadian Studies Department at Western Washington University in this lovely and historic city of Bellingham is quite probably unique among opportunities for getting personal with the Great White North among the Canadian Studies units found at various universities in the U.S.[9]

Teacher outreach, until Tina Storer arrived, was focused exclusively on the annual Study Canada Summer Institute—a weeklong course on Canada mixed with curriculum development instruction held in Canada House. Storer expanded the scope of outreach in important ways, namely by developing an impressive K–12 Teaching Canada website that displayed an array of curriculum and teaching resources, including lesson plans, teaching modules, a film and video library a student novel collection and a section on children's literature. She insisted American teachers needed to experience Canada first-hand. So, starting in 2006, the Study Canada Summer Institute was held in various Canadian cities including Vancouver, Victoria, Ottawa, and Montreal.

Storer became a national leader in promoting Canadian Studies curriculum development in state history and social studies organizations across the country. She held leadership roles in the National Council for the Social Studies and the National Council for Geographic Education and published articles on teaching Canada in national publications such as *History Matters* and the *Washington Post Education Supplement*. Her work was well known by the Canadian consular officials as she became their "go-to" speaker for teacher workshops and conferences sponsored by Canadian Consulates General in Seattle, Los Angeles, Denver, Dallas and Atlanta.

By the onset of the 21st century, Canadian–American Studies at Western was a multifaceted Center. At home, it was recognized as a major asset for the university, community, and nation. In Canada, Western was viewed as one of the few universities in the United States where serious work on relations with Canada was being done. The Canadian government underscored this point when Canadian Ambassador to the United States Raymond Chretien gave an address on Canada–U.S. relations on Western's campus on February 15, 2000—the only university stop on the itinerary of his Pacific Northwest tour.

From an academic standpoint, the Center's curriculum was well-integrated into the university's colleges and departments. The traditional areas of geography, history and political science remained robust, while considerable growth occurred in environmental studies, French language, economics and business, anthropology, journalism and the arts. Research output by Canadian–American Studies faculty increased and student enrollment in

Canadian courses was strong. Two former directors, Gerard Rutan and Bob Monahan, won the Donner Medal, a prestigious national award for outstanding achievement in Canadian Studies. The program was healthy and ready for what the new century held.

8
New Border Institute

The 9/11 Impact

Building interest in Canadian–American Studies among students and colleagues has always been difficult because Canada poses no threat to the U.S. and there are few crises. Dealings between the two countries rarely make headlines. It is true that Canadian Studies becomes more popular when significant events—not necessarily crises—dominate cross-border relations. This happened with the passage of NAFTA which, although not a crisis, marked a significant turning point in Canada–U.S. trade. It was also true when Québec held a referendum in 1995 on whether to withdraw from Canada. Few Americans would have paid attention were it not for the fact that the Québec separatists (or sovereignists—as they preferred to be known) were nearly successful. Similarly, when the Canada–U.S. border came to be viewed as problematic to the U.S. in the aftermath of September 11, 2001, Canada received a great deal of attention from Americans; ironically some was very positive as when American commercial flights in the air on September 11 were allowed to land at Gander, Newfoundland, and locals took in passengers and treated them like neighbors in need, while at the same time many Americans in the corridors of government looked warily at the relatively open Canadian border as a potential transit point for future terrorist attacks in the U.S.

Following 9/11, numerous American journalists and some

high-profile political leaders such as New York Senator Hillary Clinton claimed that the September 11 terrorists came from Canada. Even when it was established that the terrorists entered the U.S. legally on student visas, Canada was still viewed as a "weak link" in homeland security because of what many American politicians believed to be Canada's lax immigration policies. Some referred to Canadian Prime Minister Jean Chretien as "the sleepy night watchman on the northern frontier."[1]

The U.S. briefly closed all borders after 9/11 and Washington, D.C., suddenly became laser-focused on border security, both north and south. Until that time, border security was viewed mostly as a southern border issue involving undocumented immigrants and contraband coming into the U.S. from Mexico. Now, in the aftermath of 9/11, the Canada–U.S. border was deemed a serious threat to the American homeland. With this new assessment, American politicians warned that the traditional model of an undefended, generally open border was no longer valid. Now, the Canada–U.S. border would be viewed as a vulnerability in the U.S. national security system. September 11 had shifted many Americans' mindset of the border from an image of a peaceful, routine, and generally boring boundary to a northern frontier fraught with danger and threat.

The 9/11 attacks deeply affected Canadian–American Studies at Western and elsewhere in the United States. The most immediate impact came from the government's new restrictions on crossing the border. In the weeks following the attacks, border officials implemented a "total inspection" protocol which meant all vehicles would undergo full searches and travel documents would be thoroughly scrutinized. Predictably, the new security procedures caused lengthy border wait-times for commercial carriers and passenger vehicles. At Western, class visitations and other events involving Canadian professors traveling to Bellingham all but ended. Crossing the border was no longer taken for granted. Many Canadians, particularly those from visible ethnic or racial groups, refused to cross the border (some were refused entry) because of its unpredictability and outright hostility. The Association for Canadian Studies in the U.S. held its biennial conference in San

Antonio, Texas, just six weeks after 9/11. Conference attendance plummeted by more than a third because people were uncertain about, or fearful of, traveling.

The post-9/11 border was in crisis. Many inside the academic community turned their studies to examining how the border was being handled, with what consequences, and how it could be made to work better. At Western, a speakers' series was put together to discuss the new Canada–U.S. security environment. Elinor Caplan, Canada's Minister of National Revenue and Canada Customs, speaking at a campus luncheon on April 3, 2002, stressed the importance of Canadian–American Studies at this critical time and urged the university and border stakeholders—from business and local governments—to work together on border improvements. Roger Gibbins, a political scientist at the University of Calgary and CEO of the Canada West Foundation think tank, talked to classes about what he saw as the growing isolation of the U.S. as it prosecuted the war on terrorism. Lloyd Axworthy, Canada's former minister of foreign affairs, was the featured speaker during Western's Scholars Week in May of 2003. Axworthy, an internationally known Nobel Peace Prize nominee, spoke on "Human Security in a Time of Terrorism and War: A Canadian View." More than 400 people turned out for his presentation, and 150 attended a following reception. Axworthy told the audience he believed Canada–U.S. relations had entered into a new "security-first era" in which traditional relationships, business ties and friendships were being altered, possibly forever.

Locally, business groups and civic organizations worried that more restrictive security actions would cramp cross-border business activity and create economic havoc in border communities. This was not an exaggeration since much of cross-border tourism, shopping and business were concentrated in the cities and towns near the border. The Center found common cause with off-campus Canada–U.S. policy organizations such as the International Mobility & Transportation Corridor group (IMTC), a coalition of business and government agencies based in Bellingham that promoted improvements in border crossings; the Seattle-based Pacific

Northwest Economic Region (PNWER), an association of western states and Canadian provinces that fostered cross-border cooperation; and the Cascadia Center in Seattle, an organization that led regionwide efforts to improve transportation links between Oregon, Washington, and British Columbia. Concerned about the new challenges facing cross-border commerce and travelers, these groups, often with the assistance of Western faculty, pushed ideas to mitigate the damage to cross-border mobility caused by post 9/11 border security actions. Leaders throughout the Pacific Northwest were intent upon fashioning local solutions to deal with the changing politics of borders resulting from security issues now dominating Canada–U.S. relations. Canadian–American Studies already was, and would be more so in the future, an important player in this endeavor.

Border Policy Research Institute

The idea for a separate institute at Western devoted to policy research on the Canada–U.S. border began with a conversation between the university's state legislative lobbyist, Judy McNickle, and me in 2003. McNickle had become aware of a possible opportunity to secure federal funding through the office of U.S. Senator Patty Murray to develop some kind of northwest research institute at Western that would have a transportation focus. Murray, Washington state's senior senator, was the chair of the Transportation Subcommittee of the Senate Appropriations Committee, which at the time was working on a six-year transportation appropriations bill. In her position as chair of the subcommittee, she controlled discretionary spending known as "earmarks."

When McNickle contacted me, she said Murray's interest was not necessarily in the border, but more generally in policy research that would help Western, the City of Bellingham, the Port of Bellingham, and Whatcom County deal with emerging transportation issues fueled by population and trade growth, much of which was caused by increased commercial and personal travel across the border. McNickle worked closely with attorney and lobbyist

Richard (Dick) Little who did government relations work for the City of Bellingham. Little's work for the city kept him in close contact with Senator Murray, Congressman Rick Larsen, whose district extended from Everett, Washington, to the border, and Senator Maria Cantwell, Washington state's junior senator, on matters of interest to Bellingham and the northwest region of the state. Little later told me that on a trip home from D.C., he looked over a proposed list of projects in the six-year transportation bill and spotted a few that were "research of some sort." He thought, "Hey, WWU might want one."[2] Little believed that Murray would be interested in doing something for Western because of its location in a part of the state where relatively fewer federal dollars were directed (compared to Seattle and the central Puget Sound area), the university's strong program in Canadian–American Studies and the school's reputation for working with community officials in its research and outreach programs.

Western President Karen Morse was supportive of a border research institute and expressed her willingness to push the idea with Senator Murray and other members of the state's congressional delegation. Various faculty were apprised of the idea and there followed the creation of a small working group. Among the members were economists Paul Storer, Steve Globerman and Hart Hodges (Hodges was also the director of the Center for Economic and Business Research), Huxley College professor, Jean Melious, and Vice Provost for Research, Moheb Ghali. We began meeting in November 2003 to assess what might be done and who would do it. Creating a transportation institute best fit what Murray had in mind and where the funds would come from—the U.S. Department of Transportation. Members of the working group had reservations about the transportation institute idea. One concern was that Western had little expertise in transportation. A second was that federally funded transportation research centers were already operating at the University of Washington and Washington State University.

Asked by Ghali to take the lead on the initiative, which at the time was a vague concept of a transportation research institute, I strongly believed we should build on Western's strength in

Canadian–American Studies and tailor a project to fit the Canada–U.S. border. In my mind, transportation would be the major theme, but the institute we created would take advantage of our proximity to, and relationship with, Canada. I imagined the institute capitalizing on the abundant work being done at Western in the areas of Canada–U.S. trade, environment, and political and security issues—all being crucially important to maintaining and strengthening cooperative relations across the border and each directly related to transportation. An institute that dealt with transportation as well as other issues at the border would fit well with what was already occurring at Western and make it possible for the university to do something distinct from the University of Washington and other academic institutions in the region and across the country.

After discussions with the vice provost and president, we decided to move forward with a proposal for a multidisciplinary research institute—initially called The Transportation Research Institute in order to align with the major source of funding. The proposal language referred to a "broad based, analytic and future oriented institute that would take into account not only economic viability, but also critical environmental considerations." As the proposal described it, the institute:

> would develop valuable information for the public and private sector alike, as each makes decisions about the future. ... [Its] major focus would include but not be limited to critical transportation impacts associated with trade expansion, population growth, and capital investment needs in infrastructure and elsewhere, border clearance, national security, and possibly development of creative entities to facilitate international and intra-regional cooperation.[3]

The institute would draw on faculty expertise in three colleges: College of Business and Economics, Huxley College of Environmental Studies, and College of Humanities and Social Sciences. To address gaps in expertise at Western, the institute would invite research proposals and make use of knowledge from colleagues at nearby universities—in particular, the University of Washington, Washington State University, and the Center for Transportation Studies at the University of British Columbia. The institute would collaborate with the Bellingham IMTC group on specific projects related to commercial and passenger vehicle flows across the border, an area in which the IMTC had done a great deal of work. It would also work with other transportation advocacy groups such as the North Sound Connecting Communities Project ("The Farmhouse Gang"), the Cascadia Project in Seattle, and the Pacific Northwest Economic Region.

In April 2004, Dick Little and I traveled to Washington, D.C., to meet with Congressman Larsen and Senators Murray and Cantwell. The politics of the grant process required that Larsen, whose congressional district included Bellingham, sponsor the project and that Senator Cantwell also be supportive of Western's proposal. Both Larsen and Cantwell agreed to back the project, as did Bellingham's mayor, Mark Asmundsen, who had cultivated city-to-city relationships with Surrey and other B.C. municipalities near the border. A $1million appropriation for the new institute was requested for fiscal year 2005.

As the funding proposal evolved over the summer and into the fall, I thought it important to get the word "border" into the name of the institute. This would ensure that its mission would go beyond transportation to include research on issues such as cross-border security, trade, environment, and immigration.

The name change also was important because it would put the new program within the orbit of Canadian–American Studies and give Western the distinction of housing the only border research institute focused on Canada in existence in the United States. Murray's staff people were not opposed to the broader name as they saw the border as critical to transportation in our region, and so it was simply a matter of renaming the institute in different versions of the funding proposal as we went along.

In September 2004, when Murray announced inclusion of funding for Western's proposal in the appropriations budget, the name had become "Border Research Institute." Later in April 2005, when the official document awarding the grant was received by the university, the name became the "Border Policy Research Institute (BPRI)." I earlier added the word "policy" to give clear definition to the policy research function of the institute.

On September 9, 2004, Senator Murray's office sent a press release announcing that Western's proposal was among several projects in the state slated for federal funding: Western Washington University Border Research Institute—$1,000,000.

> The $1 million in FY 2005 will help establish a multi-disciplinary policy research institute at Western Washington University to develop needed information regarding transportation, mobility and border security issues for the northern corridor. WWU is at the northern terminus of the I-5 corridor and it is well situated for this project.[4]

At this point, the funding for the institute was only a recommendation from the transportation subcommittee, although Senator Murray's powerful position in the transportation appropriations process almost guaranteed a successful outcome. The final vote on the full appropriations bill was delayed on account of the November 2004 elections, but once they were over, the full bill passed congress during the end-of-year lame-duck session. The idea of a border research institute as part of Canadian programs at Western was realized.

What would it look like and who would lead it? As outlined in the proposal, the institute—now officially named the Border Policy Research Institute, or BPRI—would be a standalone entity, independent of departments and colleges, with a separate director, budget and staff. The proposal stipulated a full-time director and a full-time administrative assistant. After discussions with Vice Provost Ghali, and Provost Andrew Bodman, we decided to change the director position to half-time to make it more in line with staffing arrangements at other institutes and centers on campus. Further, should I lead the institute, as the provost anticipated, then the half time directorship of the BPRI could be conveniently joined with my existing half time directorship of the Center for

Canadian–American Studies. I was excited about the new research institute and when asked to be director, I didn't hesitate.

I was appointed director in early 2005. At that time, my position was still half time in the political science department. Now with my position changed to a 50-50 split between Canadian–American Studies and the Border Policy Research Institute, my administrative responsibilities significantly increased. I retained my position as full professor in political science and continued to teach graduate and undergraduate courses and participate in departmental business. This arrangement, splitting the directorship between the BPRI and Canadian–American Studies, appealed to Ghali and Bodman because the institute could readily draw on the resources and experience amassed in Canadian–American Studies over many years. Of course, it also simplified the hiring process.

Management of day-to-day BPRI operations would fall to an administrative assistant, later to be renamed project director, and still later, associate director. This was a critical position, especially during the start-up phase. The institute was fortunate to hire David Davidson into the position. Davidson was formerly the City Administrator of Sumas, Washington, a small city in northeastern Whatcom County located on the border. Issues related to congested border crossings were a regular part of Sumas politics and Davidson knew these issues well. Sumas was also part of a cross-border network of government bureaucrats, local businessmen and NGOs who worked on environmental and land use issues.

During Davidson's eight years working for the city, he was closely involved in these activities and knew the major players in B.C. and the central issues affecting the border. He was a quick study, deft with computer technology and an excellent communicator. Another bonus was Davidson's talent for writing short, focused policy research reports on border problems. He started a bimonthly series of "Border Policy Briefs" that diagnosed timely border issues and proposed practical solutions. These popular publications were well-liked by bureaucrats, business leaders, and other stakeholders who dealt regularly with border problems across the length of the Canada–U.S. boundary. Looking back, I am convinced it was these BPRI Border Policy Briefs probably more than anything else that quickly earned the institute a reputation as a serious, nonpartisan, evidence-based policy research organization.

The administrative office of the institute was initially located in High Street Hall next door to Canada House, and after a few months it moved across High Street to better quarters in College Hall. Following this, it moved two more times—always with a coterie of student research assistants—first to Bond Hall and then to renovated space in Miller Hall. My office remained in Canada House.

'A University Niche Program'

Initial BPRI funding was short term. The $1-million grant from the Department of Transportation stipulated a three-year time period for carrying out the project. Hoping to secure additional federal funding, President Morse, on behalf of the university, wasted no time requesting a second appropriation from Senator Murray. In March 2005, Morse made the official request:

> We are requesting $1,000,000 in the FY 2006 Transportation Appropriations bill to expand the Institute's capacity for public policy research on transportation and border issues. In recognition of the increasing importance of cross-border movement and security issues, and the need to maintain a secure and efficient transportation infrastructure on both sides of the border as we approach the 2010 Olympics in Vancouver, this appropriation would extend current research activities funded with the FY 2005 appropriation. It would also make possible a significant increase in graduate student research in the critical areas of transportation and border security.[5]

Morse's letter to Murray highlighted the significance of the upcoming 2010 Olympic and Paralympic Games to be held in Vancouver and Whistler in British Columbia. This high-profile 2010 event was already a subject of considerable interest to Washington state political leaders who were, on the one hand, worried about possible security impacts of the nearby event and, on the other hand, determined to take economic advantage of the projected surge in tourists driving up I-5 in route to Vancouver. In both cases, the condition of the border really mattered. A planning process to prepare the state for the much anticipated event was already underway. Security officials from the Washington State National Guard, the Washington State Patrol and other agencies were working closely with counterparts in B.C. and federal officials in both countries. Also involved in the planning were business groups such as chambers of commerce, and local economic development bodies as well as state and provincial tourism agencies. What they all had in common was a laser focus on a well-functioning border. Clearly, as Morse's letter to Murray suggested, the BPRI was potentially a valuable state resource to help deal with these concerns.

Following Morse's funding request, I made a trip back to Washington, D.C., to make the pitch for the second appropriation. We knew our case for new funding would be strengthened if we could show quick progress. Already in the works were several BPRI research projects. Four faculty researchers: Paul Storer (economics), Steve Globerman (economics), Hart Hodges (economics/Center for Economic and Business Research), and Jean Melious (Huxley College of the Environment) had begun research projects in summer 2005, the first undertaken by the BPRI. An inaugural Border Research Conference was held on April 26, at which an impressive lineup of border scholars and practitioners from both countries identified study areas that could form a BPRI research agenda. A BPRI external advisory board was formed and activities that partnered the BPRI with public policy organizations in Bellingham, Seattle and Vancouver were well underway. Provost Bodman in early 2005 summed up the view of the university administration that the BPRI had already made "good progress."[6]

Disappointment loomed ahead. Despite our best efforts, including letters of support from local political officials, Murray's appropriations bill for FY 2006 contained no funds for the BPRI. Congressman Larsen, after we learned the disappointing news, told me that federal dollars of the kind we received in 2005 were under greater restriction and that Western should not expect to receive additional Department of Transportation grants beyond the existing funding. Larsen said that earmarked appropriation dollars had come under more scrutiny and although they continued to be handed out in 2006, the number of grants was about 30 percent less than was the case in FY 2005. I was advised we should pursue other possibilities for federal grants—in particular the Department of Homeland Security, the Department of Justice, and the National Science Foundation. These and others were explored. However, it became apparent that most federal grant programs that had some connection to research on the Canadian border were for science, technology, and engineering projects. They did not fit the BPRI's mission of producing practical policy research.

In 2007, Bob Frazier, Western's government relations official who managed the university's interactions with legislative and agency persons in Washington, D.C., proposed creating a federally funded northern border research consortium consisting of multiple universities spanning the border from coast to coast. According to Frazier, both Senators Murray and Max Baucus of Montana had expressed interest in the consortium idea. Frazier believed joining universities from several states in a collective border research endeavor would bring visibility and political clout to northern border research upping our chances of tapping federal agencies for funding. For years there had been well funded border research institutes at several universities along the Mexican border, while none existed along the Canadian border. We believed that a northern border consortium would provide a research capability mirroring what was being done in the south.

The consortium was designed to link six universities, one in each of the main transboundary regions along the Canada–U.S. border—in order to account for the regional diversity of border-related issues—to form a comprehensive Canada–U.S. border research team. Western was the anchor for the Pacific Northwest–B.C. area and the University of Montana represented the Rocky Mountain region. Moving east, the University of North Dakota covered the Canadian prairie and U.S. northern plains, Michigan

State University and the University of Buffalo focused on the Great Lakes, and the University of Maine led the effort in the Québec–New England–Atlantic Provinces. Adjacent Canadian universities in the respective regions would be invited to participate, although they would have to secure Canadian funding. The consortium budget was set at $1 million per year for three years. Each university member would get $150,000 per year with the remaining $100,000 pooled for joint projects conducted annually. Western would lead the project and as the prime contractor would issue subcontracts to the other five institutions. Frazier was hopeful that the bulk of the money would come from the Department of Homeland Security and Department of Commerce. The BPRI drew up the design of the consortium and steered the planning, beginning with a conference held in Bellingham on January 16, 2008, at which representatives from the participating universities discussed research agendas and funding strategy.

Although a compelling idea, the consortium project was not able to get the needed funding. What went wrong? Neither Murray or Baucus ended up championing the project, making a concerted political strategy difficult. Congressional representatives in the states with participating universities, including our senators and representatives from Washington state, did little to move the project forward. Federal discretionary money needed to support the project was scarce, and would become more so as the country slipped deeper into recession in 2008. The northern border consortium project died and, with the onset of the global economic downturn, so did any realistic hopes of obtaining new federal funding for border policy research at Western.

What was needed for the long term was core state funding built into Western's regular budget. Western's administrative leaders were supportive of the BPRI, as long as it could be financed by external sources. As the prospects for federal money dimmed, the future viability of the institute was poor. Nobody really expected university officials to provide needed long-term internal support for a research institute that was not considered essential to the university's core academic operations. The Center for Canadian–

American Studies, by this time more than 30 years old, still had a paltry university funded budget and remained dependent on outside grants to sustain its non-classroom activities.

Fortuitously, events unfolded that gave the BPRI a chance to be included as a part of the university's 2006–07 biennial budget. In September 2005, Washington's Lieutenant Governor Brad Owen invited the BPRI to brief Washington state and British Columbia legislators on trade issues and border matters related to the upcoming 2010 Vancouver Olympics at a meeting of the Washington State Legislative Committee on Economic Development and International Relations, to be held at the British Columbia Parliament Building in Victoria, B.C.

Economics professor Paul Storer, probably the most knowledgeable person on the B.C.–Washington trading relationship anywhere, was the BPRI speaker. His presentation was very well received by the legislators and, most importantly, by Provost Andrew Bodman who was in attendance only because he and his wife just happened to be taking a short vacation in Victoria. Later, the provost remarked to me how his interactions with legislators in Victoria made clear to him that the BPRI was a highly valuable asset for the state because Washington's political leaders needed good, unbiased information on border and trade issues to effectively conduct economic relations with Canada. With the Vancouver Olympics coming to the region in a few years, the need for such information was ever greater. Bodman said he believe the BPRI could be a university niche program because the institute was doing something that was not being done anywhere else. Knowing that federal funding was unlikely in the long term, Bodman, upon his return to Bellingham, said he was prepared to add BPRI core funding to the university's budget request for new university programs.

The inclusion of the BPRI in the university funding package was an addition to Western's budget. Like other new budget items, it would undergo scrutiny before receiving state approval by the legislature and the governor, which was anything but a sure thing. Following the submission of the university's budget—with BPRI money included—the governor's recommendation for Western did not contain the requested funds for the BPRI. Lobbying by Representative Jeff Morris and other legislators with whom we worked closely in the Pacific Northwest Economic Region organization, and support from local State Representative Kelli Linville, later mayor of Bellingham, turned out to be crucial in getting the governor on board. When the governor's and legislature's spending recommendations were reconciled, the final budget included funding for the BPRI. Now, the institute, with a budget line of its own would become an enduring part of Canadian Studies programs at Western.

With state funding, the BPRI's future looked bright. Within two years of its creation, the BPRI had a solid track record: numerous research reports (eight underway in the first 12 months), a continuing series of bimonthly (later trimonthly) Border Policy Briefs, three significant policy-oriented conferences/symposia, frequent speaker events featuring BPRI scholars and visitors in Bellingham, Seattle, Washington, D.C., as well as other venues across the U.S. and Canada. Within this same period, BPRI staff testified at two state legislative committee hearings and one federal congressional hearing, gave border security briefings for the U.S. Department of State, and provided credible policy studies on border issues to Canadian authorities responsible for border management. An External Advisory Committee composed of academics and practitioners from both sides of the border advised on research projects, funding possibilities, and overall BPRI outreach to local and federal policy communities.

Chip Wood, the U.S. Department of Transportation administrator who was our point person in Washington, D.C., kept in close contact and let us know that the institute's work was appreciated among government officials in his department and in the Department of Homeland Security. "I've got to tell you that the January [2007] issue of the Border Policy Brief was one of the most thoughtful, informative, and useful summaries of border crossing documentation that I've seen," Wood wrote in early 2007. "I shared it with several other people here in the building and over at DHS (Department of Homeland Security) and they all agree that it was a quality piece of work. Parts of it were also incorporated into a briefing paper that I had to prepare for the Secretary."[7]

In 2006, Matt Morrison, the executive director of the Pacific Northwest Economic Region organization, approached the BPRI about signing a Memorandum of Understanding with PNWER. Morrison thought the BPRI's research capability could be a valuable addition to PNWER's work on border issues. In turn, Morrison's region-wide organization, made up of state and provincial legislators, was a political venue in which the BPRI could connect its research to key policymakers. Under the terms of the MOU, the BPRI would participate in PNWER meetings at both the staff and executive level and present research findings to its legislative membership. BPRI staff would brief legislators during annual PNWER-sponsored visits to state and provincial capitals and similar visits to Ottawa and Washington, D.C. The BPRI also would co-chair the Border Task Force at PNWER's annual summits. The arrangement provided an excellent way for the BPRI to get direct access to policymakers in the region as well as in the two federal capitals, particularly the Department of Homeland Security in D.C. and Ministry of Public Safety in Ottawa.

It is worth noting the research proposals that were funded in 2006 to get an idea of the range of topics and variety of involved faculty in the Border Policy Research Institute's early years: "An Investigation of Congestion Pricing Options for Southbound Freight at the Pacific Highway Crossing" by Mark Springer and Matt Roelofs (economics); "Risk Evaluation of Invasive Species Transport Across the U.S.–Canada Border" by Wayne Landis (Huxley College of the Environment); "Understanding the Impact of Variability in Border Crossing Times on Regional Supply Chains" by Steven Globerman (economics and Center for International Business); "Immigration Policy and Border Security, U.S. and Canada" by Bidisha Biswa (political science); "How Strategic Cross Border Business Location Decisions Impact U.S. and Canadian Economies" by Tom Dorr (economics and Small Business Development Center); "Transboundary Pollution in the Okanagan Regions of B.C. and the U.S." by Ruth Harper (Huxley College of the Environment); "Projections of Washington–British Columbia Trade and Traffic by Commodity, Route, and Border Crossing" by Washington State University economist Ken Casavant. That same year, six Border Policy Briefs and two Research Notes were published. In subsequent years, the BPRI continued to generate a steady flow of research—including masters theses and special research projects conducted by undergraduate students. Beginning in 2008, the BPRI selected annual visiting research fellows who contributed additional studies to the BPRI and became part of a cohort of border scholars that was forming at Western. By 2010, the BPRI had built an impressive track record of policy research, sustained outreach in the form of conferences and seminars, and increased involvement of Western students in a wide range of research projects.

Partnerships

From the outset, the BPRI had intended to establish research partnerships with Canadian universities. This proved difficult. Overtures were made to the Center for Transportation Studies at the University of British Columbia, but no significant partnership occurred. This was largely due to a mismatch in the missions of the BPRI and the UBC program. UBC had little interest in regional cross-border issues, aiming instead at a more global scope of work. BPRI collaboration with the University of Alberta took the form of exchanging faculty lecturers and a major grant proposal to link three universities—Alberta, Western, and Tecnologico de Monterrey, in Monterrey, Mexico—for the purpose of joining together researchers to investigate economic and security impacts stemming from U.S.–Canada and U.S.–Mexico border policies. Although the grant proposal was not funded, the planning for the project helped to widen the geographical scope of BPRI research beyond the Cascadia region.

The University of Washington, a natural U.S. partner, was home to a federally funded Washington State Transportation Research Center (TRAC) which had its own agenda and funding. Information exchanges between TRAC and BPRI staff and researchers were ongoing and one of its researchers—Professor of Civil Engineering Anne Goodchild—conducted a joint BPRI-funded research project with Western economist Steve Globerman. Farther afield, in 2008 the BPRI teamed up with the Regional Institute at the University at Buffalo to create an internet tool for measuring and publicizing changes in flows of goods and people at each major border crossing across the continent. The "Border Barometer," as it was called, was periodically updated online, notably in 2018 when the Cross-Border Institute at the University of Windsor (Ontario) was added to the research team.

The most lasting collaboration was with the University of Victoria and in particular with border expert, Emmanuel Brunet-Jailly, a faculty member in the political science department and the director of the European Union Centre for Excellence. Brunet-Jailly is a prominent border scholar and a leader in the Association for Borderland Studies, the preeminent academic association that focuses on border studies. Western and Victoria launched their collaboration with a noteworthy two-university binational conference that was held in both Victoria, B.C., and Bellingham in January, 2008.

The 2008 Victoria–Bellingham conference was organized under the auspices of the Border Regions in Transitions organization. BRIT is an international scientific meeting of interdisciplinary scholars who convene every eighteen months to share research on issues facing cross-border regions throughout the world. BRIT conferences are traditionally hosted jointly by two universities located on each side of an international border. The 2008 conference, with venues in Victoria in B.C. and Bellingham in Washington, highlighted the particularities of the Cascadia region and the distinctive international marine boundary dividing Canada and the United States. Conferees experienced firsthand the unique geography of the boundary and the legendary northwest winter weather when they were transported by boat from Victoria to Bellingham across the Salish Sea during a January rainstorm. As the boat pitched in the gale-driven waves, and most of the professors were hunkered down, a contingent of Finnish scholars, well plied with beer, assured me and others still upright that this was "nothing" compared to what they routinely experienced in the North Atlantic.

The BRIT conference served to solidify a cross-border academic partnership between the two universities. This collaboration has continued to the present day. Western signed an MOU with Victoria in 2012 as one of several university partners in a multimillion dollar Borders in Globalization grant from the Canadian Social Science and Humanities Research Council. In 2017, Victoria and Western entered into a formal visiting scholar agreement where border scholars from around the world annually divide research visits between both universities.

9
A House Matters

CanAm: The New Millennium

While the BPRI was being established as the first border research institute on the northern border, the Canadian–American Studies academic program grew in scope and depth. By 2010 one or more well-trained Canadianists were in place in nearly all departments in the social sciences and humanities. The economics department was especially strong with Paul Storer and Steve Globerman, both experts on Canadian economic policy and Canada–U.S. trade, complemented by Ross Professors James Dean and Stephen Blank. In the history department, Cecilia Danysk taught five Canadian history courses, the most offered by any Canadian Studies program in the United States. The geography program received a boost in 2006 with the hiring of David Rossiter, a recent Ph.D. from York University in Toronto, who specialized in Canadian cultural and historical geography. Canadian Francophone language and cultural studies were buttressed in the French program with the hiring of Christina Keppie, a specialist in Acadian language and culture. As it turned out, two of these individuals would go on to become directors of the Center—David Rossiter from 2014 to 2018 and Christina Keppie, the first woman to hold the position, took the reins in 2018.

The curriculum was continually refreshed by visiting faculty, in particular the holders of the Ross and Canadian Culture professorships and, beginning in 2004, annual visiting professors from Québec. New courses were cycled into the curriculum by the offering of specialized classes and seminars. Examples included Cecilia Danysk's honors seminar, "Nationalism in the French Canadian Context" and two specialized courses in the English Department offered by Nancy Pagh, "The World of Emily Carr" and "Women in Literature." Exploring regional cross-border literature was the theme of Pagh's "Writing in Context" course, which featured class visits by writers from both sides of the border. Two field courses on borderlands were offered by geographer Patrick Buckley and anthropologist James Loucky respectively. Both courses connected students personally—through field visits and border spanning classes—with cultural communities, political leaders, and academics in neighboring Richmond and Abbotsford, two of the most culturally diverse cities in British Columbia.

By 2010, Canadian–American Studies offered a pan-Canadian curriculum, blending a comprehensive focus on the Canadian nation as a whole along with emphasis on the regions of Québec, the Western provinces, and particularly British Columbia. Western's political scientists and economists focused on Canadian political and economic structures as well as Canada–U.S. political and economic relations. The latter topic incorporated a wide range of material dealing with border studies. The centrality of Indigenous peoples to Canadian history and modern life was addressed in several anthropology and Fairhaven College courses about Native and First Nations peoples of North America. Specialized history classes dealt with Canadian immigrants, women in Canadian history, New France, Canadian labor, and rural Canada. Courses on the culture and French language of Québec were integrated into the French program. The English department had a special topics course focused on Canadian literature, and Canadian art history was incorporated into offerings in the art department. In Huxley College of the Environment, several courses on Canadian environmental history, geography and policy were available. Few, if any, schools in the U.S. could match the comprehensiveness of Western's undergraduate Canadian–American Studies offerings.

In 2002, the major was revised to offer two tracks. Track One was called Canadian–American Studies with French Language. This track, mostly unchanged from the traditional major, required several first-, second-, and third-year French language courses. Students typically combined it with French as a second major. Track Two was called Canadian–American Studies with Area of Concentration. Students in this track selected a subject area such as political science, environmental studies, or economics, for example, and took courses in that area in consultation with an advisor. The number of required credits in both tracks was kept relatively low to encourage double majors. For completion of both tracks, students were required to take the multidisciplinary gateway course, Can/Am 200 (Introduction to Canadian Studies), and the senior-level tutorial research courses, Can/Am 401 and 402. The number of students who completed a major in the field averaged between six and 10 per year. The number of minors was considerably larger. While the number of majors was small, each year several hundred students took Canadian Studies courses as part of their general education. This served a fundamental purpose of the Center; to expose as many Western students as possible to Canadian Studies subject matter.

Faculty research output was steady. A list of the books, peer-reviewed articles and reports published would fill several pages and is not included here. As well, most Center faculty were active in presenting research at conferences in their respective disciplines and at Canadian Studies conferences such as the Association of Canadian Studies in the United States, the Western Social Science Association, and the Association of Canadian Studies in Canada. Three directors received the coveted Donner Medal for outstanding scholarship and service in Canadian Studies: Gerard Rutan in 1987, Robert Monahan in 1999, and I received the medal in 2007.

The program manager position changed in 2003. Paul "Chuck" Hart, formerly on the staff of the University Housing and Residences office was hired into the position when Marty Hitchcock, finishing her 10th year in Canada House, moved on to work in the accounting department in the College of Business and

Economics. Chuck's university experience was extensive, dating back to when he was a student in the political science department followed by many years as an administrator in the student housing office. His familiarity with campus organization proved to be beneficial for navigating the always growing university bureaucracy. His sunny demeanor brought compliments from the likes of diplomats, legislators, business leaders and assorted visitors who did business with the Center. He knew every Canadian–American Studies student and, as the only administrative staff person for the program, he eagerly took on the roles of guidance counselor and trusted friend to the students.

The Center had always benefitted from support from Canadian Consuls General (and their staffs) who typically served three-year terms at the Consulate General of Canada in Seattle. Never were we more fortunate than when Roger Simmons was appointed to the Consul General post in 1998. Simmons, a native of the province of Newfoundland and Labrador, had been a school teacher before winning elected offices to the provincial legislature and then to the Canadian House of Commons. As Consul General, he seemed to be in perpetual motion explaining the importance of Canada to all manner of American audiences ranging from children in grade schools to elected political leaders. His ability to 'work the room' was legendary. I recall one occasion when after he gave a lecture to a large introductory class on Canada, Simmons strolled up and down the lecture hall aisles buttonholing students and handing out his business cards to them, most of whom were freshmen and sophomores. His support for our program was absolute. On his first trip north to Bellingham after assuming his post in Seattle, he made a point to make an unannounced visit to Canada House before his scheduled meetings with city and county government officials, explaining that he had heard "this is where the important educational work on Canada–U.S. relations is happening so I needed to come here first." Simmons was aided by a particularly effective team that included Consul Kim Blanchette, Political/Economic Officer, Patrick Higgins and Academic Relations and Public Affairs Officer, Kevin Cook.

During the early 2000s, student exchanges and internships increased, but not to the extent we hoped for. Most student exchanges with Canadian universities were arranged through the International Student Exchange Program, a worldwide network of universities that included many in Canada. Several students worked out their own study abroad arrangements at various Canadian campuses, most commonly the University of Alberta and the University of British Columbia. A bilateral exchange agreement was signed with Trent University in Peterborough, Ontario, focused on environmental studies in 2003, but, lacking the attraction of a more cosmopolitan area, and without student scholarships as incentives, the university in Peterborough did not appeal to Western students.

Closer to home, the exchange with SFU was still drawing students but the numbers were low. An agreement to promote student exchanges, faculty visits and research in cross-border resource management was signed with the University College of the Fraser Valley in Abbotsford, B.C., in 2006. But interest waned and except for the continuation of the UCFV–WWU cross-border course taught by geography professor Patrick Buckley, nothing came of it. More popular were student internships arranged with government agencies, such as ministries in the B.C. government, the U.S. and Canadian Consulates General in Vancouver and Seattle, PNWER, the Whatcom Council of Governments, and other entities within easy driving distance from Bellingham. Internships, unlike exchanges, were mostly ad hoc, organized on a case-by-case basis. It was always perplexing to me why students seemed to lack interest in studying at a Canadian university. One apparent factor was the perception that Canada was not "different enough" from the United States. Québec was more alluring and several students ventured off each summer to study in the province's French-language programs. It is likely students' lack of interest in Canadian universities is, at least in part, a function of the reluctance of American students to study abroad in general. A 2018 study in *University World News* reported that, compared to students in Canada, U.K., New Zealand, and Australia, American students are the least likely to cross borders to study for a degree.

In 2003, the Center began working with the Government of Québec to set up an annual visiting professorship in Québec Studies at Western. The initiative had its roots in Québec's growing economic and cultural diplomacy in the United States. The Québec Ministry of International Relations was interested in strengthening its business and cultural contacts with West Coast states, particularly California, but also Oregon and Washington. A significant technology connection had developed between Québec and American tech companies such as Microsoft and Google. Trade and energy ties between Québec and Western states were increasing as well. As part of its diplomatic efforts to better inform Americans about Québec society and politics, the Québec government launched educational initiatives at a few U.S. universities where faculty were engaged in teaching and research on Canada. Western's program was on Québec's radar screen because of its comprehensive focus on Canada, its Québec courses in the French department, and its record of business outreach with firms and local governments. Another factor was Québec officials, like those in other provinces, were concentrating on border policy after 9/11 and the BPRI offered a model of successful collaborative policy research between adjacent provinces and states. For these reasons, and the fact that the new head of the Québec Government Office in Los Angeles, Marc Boucher, had academic ties with a few of Western's faculty, the French-speaking province was interested in establishing a visiting Québec scholar program with Western that would also include the University of Washington.

With strong support from Marc Boucher, the program began in 2004 with a grant of $41,500 from the Québec government. The funding was intended to cover the salary and travel for an annual visiting scholar to be based in Bellingham for one term. That individual would also travel to the University of Washington to give seminars and guest lectures and teach a course if funding and logistics permitted. The guidelines stipulated that the visiting scholar teach one course, give lectures to business groups and other universities, do interviews with the media and promote study-in-Québec opportunities for Western and University of Washington students.

During the seven years of the program's existence, six visiting scholars taught at Western. The course offerings varied, though most dealt with Québec political studies. A valuable relationship developed between Western and the University of Québec at Montreal—where a number of visiting scholars came from—that continued even after the program ended. Led by Frederick Gagnon, a UQAM professor who taught and conducted research on Québec politics while a visiting professor at Western, and later hosted the Study Canada Summer Institute when it was held in Montreal, UQAM scholars were (and continue to be) an enduring source of expertise on Québec Studies in the Pacific Northwest.

In 2006, the *American Review of Canadian Studies*, the multidisciplinary academic journal for ACSUS, was looking for a new editor and new university home base. At that time, the journal was under the editorship of Mark Kasoff, a professor of economics at Bowling Green State University in Ohio. I believed the time was opportune for Canadian–American Studies to make a bid for the editorship of the journal. For one thing, ARCS was the largest Canadian Studies journal in the world and its presence at Western would add an important intellectual dimension to the Center. As well, the journal—exclusively located in the eastern part of the country—would benefit from being based in the West. In supporting Western's bid for ARCS, Provost Andrew Bodman pointed out how the journal and the broader Canadians Studies community in the U.S. could profit from being connected to Western's Center:

> We at Western Washington University are strongly committed to the development of Canadian Studies in the United States and believe that a strong national journal is a critical element in this mission. ... As you know, the university's is a Title VI National Resource Center and we recently received substantial funding for the new Border Policy Research Institute. The university believes the *American Review of Canadian Studies* can benefit by our rapidly expanding Center and sharper focus on Canada–U.S. border issues.[1]

To bring the journal to Western, there needed to be a qualified faculty member ready to serve as editor. We were fortunate that Dr. John Purdy, a professor in the English department whose courses and National Science Foundation workshops dealt with Native American literature, expressed interest in the position. Purdy's teaching and research for the past 20 years had focused on the Indigenous literatures of the Western Hemisphere. He had considerable experience with editorial work, including seven years as editor of the scholarly quarterly, *Studies in American Indian Literature*. Previous to this, Purdy worked as Associate Editor for Fiction and Native Poetry for *Calapooya Collage*, a publication that featured writings by Native authors from around the globe. Purdy's work fit well with the interdisciplinary nature of ARCS and the growing interest in Native American and First Nations writings, which had heretofore been scarce in the journal. A funding package was worked out with the provost and with the approval of the ARCS editorial board, Purdy was appointed editor. Purdy received some release time from teaching and was assisted by a Managing Editor, Kathy Reigstad, who had extensive experience as an independent editor for several major publishing companies.

ARCS moved to Western in 2006 and was a feature of the Center for the next 12 years. Purdy was editor for four years, succeeded by Geography Professor David Rossiter who held the position from 2011–2015. In 2010, Catherine Wallace, who had a background in journalism, independent editorial and graphic design, and also taught writing at Western and journalism at Whatcom Community College, took over as Managing Editor. French Professor Christina Keppie was appointed editor in 2015 and served through 2018 when ARCS was moved to a new home at Bridgewater State University in Massachusetts. The move was prompted by a tradition of rotating the editorship and Keppie's new responsibilities as director of Western's Center.

The Canadian–American Studies mission of educating students, K–12 teachers and the broader public seemed assured even as the trends in scholarship nationally were moving away from traditional area studies programs to more vocationally oriented pursuits such as technology and engineering. The multifaceted nature of Western's Canadian programs provided a growing and unmatched base of expertise in the northwest corner of the state. In this regard, as was noted by an evaluation team in 2012, "Can-Am Studies at Western has been a pioneer in shifting to a role as a locus or hub of resources in support of faculty and students across campus," and, through extensive public outreach and the work of the BPRI, it has "bridged the gap between study and practitioners that confound many universities."[2]

Indeed, as a "hub of resources" the Center provided academic and public outreach services that went far beyond what could have been imagined back at the time of its founding in 1971. What is true is that by the end of the first decade of the 21st century, Canadian–American Studies evolved into a place for multidisciplinary teaching and research on all facets of Canada, for border policy, for operating a nationally recognized curriculum program for K–12 educators and for influencing the state's and nation's diplomatic activities with Canada. Each of the program components interrelate and together they had become a major scholarly asset for the campus, the state and nation.[3]

Our efforts to strengthen the Center were helped by the long-standing partnership between our program and the Canadian Studies Center at the University of Washington, a bond greatly fortified when Nadine Fabbi became managing director of the UW center in 1999. The two programs, different as they were, managed to achieve a high degree of unity in K–12 outreach while manifesting different areas of expertise on Canada. Western had developed particular strengths in border studies, environmental policy and Canada–U.S. business and economic matters. UW's Arctic studies and Indigenous languages programs were notable as was the institution's policy research in professional schools such as forestry and public health. As a single Pacific Northwest consortium, the range and depth of resources focused on Canada were all encompassing. I think it is fair to say that the WWU–UW consortium more than fulfilled the expectations of its founders—Robert Monahan and Douglas Jackson—when the two Pacific Northwest universities first teamed up in 1986.

Canada House Redux

While Westerns's Canadian–American Studies programs were doing well, Canada House still faced an uncertain future because university administrators could not decide what to do with it. To my continuing surprise, few presidents seemed to appreciate the building's historical and political significance and its potential for Western. Even former President Olscamp, who in the 1970s had been the main force in making Canada House the Center's home in the first place, did not defend the building from takeover by the Faculty Club.

In 2000, the Center became aware of a proposal in the university's Institutional Master Plan to tear down the building to make room for a larger parking lot and a bus turnaround. When word got out about this, numerous faculty, some of whom had little or no connection with Canadian–American Studies, sent letters of protest. The idea that an historic building, which for more than 20 years housed an academic program and hosted a wide range of Canadian and American leaders, would be destroyed to expand parking seemed to many rightfully outrageous.

"The scheme seems to me ill-considered," wrote Milt Krieger, a professor in the Liberal Studies department, in a letter to the president. Krieger said he thought that Canadian–American Studies and its building, Canada House, go hand in hand. He lauded the program for its achievements and suggested that having its own site was vital because it afforded independence from any department which encouraged interdisciplinary teaching and research. Krieger went on to say that the particular site for the program's building mattered a lot:

> The building's north facing view to the waters and mountains linking us to and defining Canada is a powerful sign to all those connected with the program on campus, and even more to those interested parties off campus, and indicates Western's real advantage and serious purpose in the enterprise.[4]

English Professor Nancy Pagh wrote President Morse about

how important "place" is for fostering the program's identity. She wrote, "As an interdisciplinary scholar, I know that it is crucial—but extremely difficult—to create a common identity for an interdisciplinary program such as Canadian–American Studies." Pagh then got to the heart of the matter:

> Experience has taught me that a place, a site, is absolutely essential to establish and maintain that sense of identity. Having Canada House as a site for the program's identity means more than having a place where students in the program can go for support. It is the one place where diverse faculty participants share common ground, both literally and figuratively.

Like Krieger, Pagh pointed to the importance of the physical site itself because of what it meant for the community's relationship with Canada:

> The building itself matters to the program and to Western. Canada House, as a site, announces that we as a community take Canada seriously; this announcement is made through the name of course, but also through the longevity of the site and from its position—which looks directly to the mountains of British Columbia.[5]

The letters appeared to have made a difference. Provost Bodman wrote to me on November 21, 2000, stating, "I have succeeded in removing the reference to the demolition of Canada House from the latest draft of the Institutional Master Plan."[6] Morse insisted that the issue was overblown and that the reference to the building in the Master Plan was nothing more than part of the advisory committee's deliberations on many options being considered in the overall plan.[7]

Whatever fate might have awaited Canada House, the building escaped the wrecking ball, at least for the time being. But its deteriorating condition was another problem altogether. The house was badly in need of repair and a coat of paint. The downstairs rooms had taken a beating from continued use, and too much abuse, from the Faculty Club's Friday socials and other activities. Even getting the building upgraded for wireless internet service proved to be an ordeal as we were repeatedly told that Canada House was not listed in campus planning documents as official academic space, and thus could not get needed infrastructure until this designation was changed.[8]

In 2002, I made a formal request to the vice president in charge of the campus physical plant for some needed office improvements, including full access to internet service. My request was modest, certainly far short of asking for a renovation of Canada House in keeping with its original elegance (although I hoped this could be done some day); only that the university commit to repairs and upgrades befitting the house's purpose and symbolism. The response was short and direct: budget restraints would only allow the most basic level of maintenance.

In 2008, buoyed by the BPRI's growing reputation off campus and the growth of the Canadian–American Studies academic program and K–12 outreach, it seemed an auspicious time to again try to persuade university officials to finally do something about the deteriorating condition of Canada House. In discussions with local businessman Craig Cole, a former chair of Western's Board of Trustees, an idea was conceived to seek funding to upgrade Canada House so it could better support routine academic operations and also serve as a dignified place where government and business leaders could congregate to deal with cross-border problems. In a letter to President Morse, I described the idea:

> In effect, [the house] could be a neutral center for problem solving…The increased interaction among Canadian and U.S. organizations and groups up and down the Cascadia Corridor is remarkable and WWU, with an established Canadian Center with a great reputation, is well-positioned to serve as a focal point for all kinds of activities…[9]

My thinking was Canada House was already being used by government, NGO and business leaders as a geographically convenient and politically impartial setting for seminars and meetings addressing Canada–U.S. trade problems, environmental concerns and border matters, so why not officially bolster what was already being done? With a more public purpose, college administrators might be more inclined to upgrade the building. I had in mind a model similar to the Ruckleshaus Center, jointly operated by the University of Washington and Washington State University, which served to facilitate private and public sector leaders coming together to solve problems in areas such as health care, land use and conservation. Canada House seemed ideal as a site for this kind of public outreach and problem solving in the B.C.–Washington cross-border region. These activities would be enriched by the Center's corps of expert faculty and enthusiastic students who would in turn benefit a great deal by interacting with regional leaders.

Before such a plan could be carried out, the building would need to undergo significant renovations to improve its appearance, refurbish seminar and other public spaces and add appropriate furnishings and media/communications infrastructure. The estimated price tag was $900,000.

President Morse liked the idea in principle, although not so much that she would commit money from Western's capital budget. A funding strategy was devised to work with political allies outside the university to try to get the needed money added to the state's capital budget, while also approaching private funders. Craig Cole agreed to help with the campaign. He was well connected with local and state political leaders and was at the time the chair of the University of Washington Board of Regents. Various legislators, most notably Jeff Morris—a state legislator from Mt. Vernon in Skagit County south of Bellingham, who was also Speaker Pro Tempore of the state House of Representatives and had been influential in getting state funding for the BPRI—pushed the effort at the level of the governor's office. Bellingham Mayor Dan Pike and Whatcom County Executive Pete Kremen wrote in support of the project. Cole personally asked the presidents from Western and UW if they could support the funding request and both said yes, although saying yes is different than fighting for it. It is not known how much fight went into the effort. Nonetheless, with crucial help from a small group of state legislators, the budget item for the renovation made it into the state's Proposed 2009–2011 Biennial Capital Budget, passed by the House Capital Budget Committee, as one of 19 projects in the state.

Private sector donors were approached but only one gave a firm commitment. Puget Sound Energy was willing to contribute retrofitting the building's windows to a high level of energy efficiency, an action that would fit with Western's sustainability goals to which PSE had contributed.

When the governor's final budget was released, the Canada House funding was not part of it. Support from the House Capital Budget Committee was not sufficient to overcome broader political and economic interests vying for state government funding. Looking back, it is a wonder the funding request got as far as it did, considering the campus's other capital needs and the university administration's general indifference to Canada House. Although Western's administrators were willing to go along with the Canada House project as long as private funding would materialize, there was never a chance they would make it a university budget priority.

A larger reality was that Canada House, and for that matter the Canadian–American Studies Program as a whole, lacked consistent champions in Western's leadership ranks. Interest in Canadian programs by presidents, provosts, and deans waxed and waned over the years. Perhaps this is the fate of interdisciplinary programs everywhere, and it certainly was the case in this highly departmentalized university. Despite continual talk about the Canadian programs being a distinctive feature of Western, successive administrations adopted, for the most part, a laissez-faire approach to the Center and the facility in which it was housed.

A few years later Canada House dodged what would have been a fatal bullet. In the Western's Capital Budget request for 2013–2015, Canada House was slated for demolition to make way for an expansion of the Performing Arts Center (located next door) and the construction of a new academic services building to be known as the Gateway Complex. The die was cast for this project so no amount of protesting from Canadian–American Studies allies or even outside intervention from people hoping to designate the House an 'historic place' would likely make any difference. This time Canada House was saved only because the always budget minded state legislature refused to fund the proposed Performing Arts Center/Gateway Complex project.

Canada House remained the home of the Center and the location for the Faculty Club's Friday afternoon cocktail parties, while the BPRI was housed in various offices in other buildings. The dust would finally settle in 2015 when the Faculty Club, much diminished in size and influence from earlier years, was moved out of Canada House as part of an overall reorganization of Canadian programs and the Center was given control of the entire building. Canadian–American Studies, the BPRI and the newly established Salish Sea Institute were consolidated in Canada House. Finally, the building was being used in a way that I and other colleagues had long hoped for.

The Great Recession

The economic downturn in late 2007 and the national recession that followed hit Western hard. By 2010, when the full force of the calamity impacted the state budget, the state had a shortfall of nearly $1.5 billion. The result was that Western took major state budget cuts as did the other public universities in the state. Since the lion's share of the university budget is in faculty salaries, either tenured faculty would have to be laid off or the money would come from somewhere else. From the administration's vantage, the obvious and I think appropriate decision was to preserve full-time faculty and look for cuts in other areas.

I knew that Canadian–American Studies and the BPRI were vulnerable because the two programs lacked the protection that comes from being an academic department with regular tenured faculty. Also, there were changes in the top leadership of the university following President Morse's retirement and Provost Bodman's move to another university in California. In 2008, Bruce Shepard, formerly the Chancellor of the University of Wisconsin–Green Bay was appointed president. Shepard had West Coast roots having received all of his higher education in the University of California system, taught political science at Oregon State University for 23 years and served as provost at Eastern Oregon University before moving to Wisconsin. Catherine Riordan, a professor of psychology and, prior to coming to Western, the vice provost at Central Michigan University, was named provost in 2009. Both the new president and provost showed little interest in Canadian–American Studies when they arrived at Western. With budget cuts looming because of the recession, they had a laser-like focus on protecting academic departments.

When Provost Riordan called me in one day to talk about cuts, I expected to be told our budgets would be reduced by at least 7 percent, the number that most departments were expecting, and probably much higher. Riordan said that her responsibility was to protect the academic core of the university, and though Canadian–American Studies and the BPRI were important in her view, they were not part of the core. That said, I could not have been prepared for what came next. She told me I would need to reduce our programs' combined budgets by $150,000—a full 44 percent of our state-funded monies. My response to her was one of incredulity. "It sounds like you are trying to kill the Canadian programs," I said with an edge of anger. Her response was no, if killing the programs was her intent, she would have told me straightaway. After assuring me the cuts were nonnegotiable, the provost then put it on me to determine how the cuts would be implemented—which was certainly better than letting her decide the matter. The Canadian–American Studies budget was $165,413; the BPRI budget was $225,416. The director salary and those for David Davidson and Chuck Hart, were counted in the figures. My salary was protected because I retained my position as a tenured faculty member in the political science department. I was not going to eliminate either of the other positions because the staff, already small, was vital to the programs' survival. And, I had no intention of cutting anyone's salary. What I did was carve the amount requested from two principal areas: From the Canadian–American Studies budget, the half-time faculty salary line for the Distinguished Professor of

Canadian Culture was eliminated,[10] and from the BPRI budget, research and operations funds were essentially cut in half.

With other funding sources—grant funds and self-sustaining revenue accumulated from interest on endowments—Canadian–American Studies could shoulder on. The Title VI grant, although reduced because of recessionary cuts in federal programs, kept Canadian–American Studies functioning. Annual grants from the Government of Canada had been vital in supporting faculty travel, conferences and symposia, and some Center program operations in the past. However, almost as if a perfect storm had set upon us, these grants were eliminated by the Canadian government in 2011. With the loss of funding for the distinguished professor position, the Center had no means to pay short-term visiting faculty and speakers in the area of cultural studies. The K–12 outreach program, and particularly Tina Storer's salary and the annual Study Canada Summer Institute, were less affected because they were funded almost entirely by federal dollars.

As for the BPRI, its research and operations budget was cut by 50 percent. Now, with half as much state funding, the institute supported far fewer faculty research projects and the visiting border fellows program was eliminated. Fortunately, government and business leaders on both sides of the border put a high value on BPRI research, and stepped up with small grants for specific projects. Such projects included gathering and analyzing data on border operations to help local governments influence federal and state authorities to make changes in future investments in infrastructure. The BPRI also conducted several research projects focused on the new Beyond the Border Action Plan announced by President Obama and Canadian Prime Minister Harper in 2011. The BPRI continued to arrange conferences and symposia on border issues in partnership with a variety of organizations, most notably the Woodrow Wilson Center for International Scholars in D.C., Canadian Consulates General in Seattle and Dallas, and the Vancouver Board of Trade. Seven such meetings were convened between 2009–2012.

I strongly believed then and now that the Canadian programs

had to carry an unfair portion of the university's revenue reductions. I was disappointed in the provost's decision because she seemed to have acted impulsively without considering the equitability or program impacts of what she was doing. Happily, even with the severe budget cuts, the Canadian programs at Western did not fade away, or reduce their scope of activities as much as first seemed likely.

Diminished BPRI money for faculty research meant more in-house research would be conducted by BPRI staff—mostly by David Davidson and whatever graduate and undergraduate research assistants he could enlist—frequently in collaboration with government agencies with border management responsibilities. The Can-Am teaching program remained mostly intact because tenured Canadian–American Studies affiliated faculty (all in the regular departments) were little affected by the cuts. Courses traditionally taught by visiting faculty (except the Ross professors) were all but eliminated. And, the funding for the half time position for the Distinguished Professor of Canadian Culture was taken away. When the economic downturn ended, the money that was cut from Canadian Studies program budgets was not restored.

10
A Border Runs Through It

As has been discussed throughout this book, the border is a constant theme in all facets of Canadian Studies at Western. It is essential to the geographical space we inhabit and it has persistent effects on the economic and cultural life of the Northwest region. The border's most obvious effect is to differentiate the Canadian nationality from that of the United States. But it is meaningful in so many other ways. The border has always been a site of struggle for Indigenous peoples who resist being enclosed within boundaries drawn by colonial powers. The border is a security fence but it also is a gateway for immigrants, commerce, travel and family interaction. As a political division the border complicates the management of border straddling wilderness areas, airsheds, water systems, and pandemics. With the unfolding of the second decade of the 21st century, the border continued to animate the work of Western's Canadian Studies programs, and in a few years, another border-related institute would be created within Canada House.

It's All About the Border

During the years following 9/11, concerns about dangerous people and contraband crossing the border dominated Canada–U.S. relations. Both countries strengthened security regulations, impeding the daily cross-border movement of approximately $2 billion in goods and services. The cost to both producers and consumers was enormous, with a large portion of it borne by companies, retail outlets, and tourism operations in border-region communities such as Bellingham. Personal travel and related social interaction plummeted as well. Even more alarming was the growing militarization of the border. Federal authorities in Washington, D.C., increased the number of agents at the northern border from about 300 to more than 2,000 between 2001 and 2010. The legendary "longest undefended border in the world" was transformed into a semi-militarized zone of high-tech air and on-the-ground surveillance gadgetry to complement the operations of the greatly expanded Border Patrol.

From the standpoint of border policy, the Bush Administration after 9/11 was quick to tighten border security at both the Canadian and the Mexican borders. Heightened security was the purpose of the "Smart Borders" agreement between the U.S. and Canada signed in December 2001, and the U.S.–Mexico Border Partnership Agreement enacted in 2002. Both accords prioritized security, but they also aimed to make sure cross-border commerce and travelers were not hopelessly bottlenecked. This changed in 2005 with the appointment of the second head of the U.S. Department of Homeland Security, Michael Chertoff, who understood his job as making sure that another 9/11 would never happen. To this end, he oversaw an inflexible "security first" approach to managing the border, with almost no regard to the costs of disrupting flows of cross-border trade and people.

Border policy changed somewhat in 2011 when President Barack Obama and Canadian Prime Minister Stephen Harper signed a new accord designed to make the border crossings less burdensome without compromising security. The accord, titled "Beyond the Border: A Shared Vision for Perimeter Security and Economic Competition" focused on securitizing flows of goods and people before they entered and moved across North America. In this different way of thinking, inspecting a container on a freighter leaving, say, Shanghai bound for the United States was just as essential as inspecting a truck entering the country at a Canada–U.S. border crossing. Under the new strategy "securing the border" would prioritize checking people, cargo, and baggage in transit before they reached the U.S.–Canada territorial boundary. In this way, much of the traffic arriving at border crossings would already be pre-checked, thereby speeding up the movement of goods and travelers once they reached inspection stations at Blaine and other entry points along the northern border. The accord also aimed to improve collaboration between Canadian and U.S. border agents and law enforcement officials and streamline border infrastructure and customs operations at all border crossings.

More so than in the first few years following 9/11, policy officials responsible for border policy became interested in academic policy research that could help achieve the goal of ensuring that commerce and people could move efficiently across the border while maintaining necessary levels of security. Unlike the top-down, "Washington, D.C., knows best" approach evident during the Chertoff years, implementation of the Beyond the Border accord involved conducting local pilot projects and working with stakeholders in border communities. As one of the only policy institutes in existence with a focus on the northern border, and situated at the heart of the third busiest Canada–U.S. border crossing, the Border Policy Research Institute was positioned to provide needed expertise.

The BPRI had already developed an impressive network of relationships with state and federal officials, stakeholders, and Canadian and U.S. border agents crucial for data collection and conducting field research. These relationships went beyond the local level, and extended up to policy leaders in the two national capitals, including Canadian Ambassador to the U.S. Michael Wilson who visited Western on December 11, 2007 to be briefed on border issues impacting the Cascadia Corridor region. In September of 2009, following President Obama's appointment of David Jacobson to be the new U.S. Ambassador to Canada, the Department of State invited BPRI Associate Director David Davidson to Washington, D.C., to give the ambassador a closed, off-the-record briefing on the Canada–U.S. border. Later, in June of 2011 during a visit to Western, Jacobson met with BPRI researchers to discuss findings from their studies that showed how truck delays could be reduced at the border crossing in Blaine, Washington.

The BPRI became an outlet for policy research for the Beyond the Border accord and produced numerous reports and briefs that helped the Beyond the Border Working Group—the body assigned to implement the accord—to devise ways to improve border crossings and be responsive to the concerns and interests of people in local border communities. Some examples of this research illustrate what was being done: "Metrics of Policy Effects at the Canada–U.S. Border" (2012); "Is RFID the Answer to Resurgent Border Traffic" (2012); "Federal Initiatives Can Be at Odds With Regional Ones" (2013); "The Pre-Inspection Pilot Test at Blaine: Field Data" (2013); "Pilot Project: Using RFID to Reduce Border Queues" (2014). Data-driven studies of this kind depended on close cooperation between BPRI researchers and on-the-ground officials at the border inspection stations.

United States Consul General Anne Callaghan, based in Vancouver, B.C., recognized as much when she remarked, "when you see a group like Western Washington University's Border Policy Research Institute work as closely as they do with CBP [Customs and Border Protection] to come up with data based solutions that benefits everyone, you know something is working right."[1] On all of these research projects, Western students were employed to conduct fieldwork at the border crossings in Whatcom County. Through this experience, the students gained useful research skills by interviewing drivers, tabulating wait-time information and organizing and assessing data. Some obtained internships and others went on to find jobs in organizations with border policy responsibilities. The BPRI had become a well-known and highly respected research arm of Canadian–American Studies activities at Western.

Organizing conferences and seminars to exchange policy ideas with border stakeholders and to seek their input was always a part of the BPRI's stock in trade, and more so as new border policy changes were rolled out by the U.S.–Canada Beyond the Border Working Group. By 2012, the Working Group had developed numerous border initiatives of direct interest to the Pacific Northwest region. Among these were expanding lanes that can accommodate NEXUS travelers at the main border crossings in Whatcom County; making business travel easier by incorporating business "expedited crossing" documentation into the NEXUS program; easing truck congestion by reducing documentation required by customs and other agencies; and speeding up southbound Amtrak trains by moving security inspections from the border in Blaine to the Vancouver, B.C. train station. In partnership with the Consulate General of Canada, the BPRI organized a conference at the World Trade Center in Seattle on February 10, 2012, to discuss these and other issues with federal officials. The conference was designed to solicit local public input to ensure that regional border concerns were taken into account as new Beyond the Border policy ideas were brought forward. Later that year, on October 24, 2012, the BPRI teamed up with the Vancouver Board of Trade to cosponsor a similar one-day conference at the Fairmont Hotel Vancouver to give feedback to Ottawa officials in charge of border policy. This kind of ongoing outreach, intrinsic to the BPRI mission, has contributed to the regional cooperation that has been a hallmark of the Cascadia area.

As well, the local and national media utilized BPRI studies. When a bridge on the I-5 freeway in Mt. Vernon, Washington collapsed on May 24, 2013, after its support structure was hit by a truck, there was widespread concern about the economic effects of a rupture in the main transportation link between British Columbia and California. Dozens of news outlets in Canada, Washington State, Oregon and California, used BRPI research to understand how commercial traffic up and down the West Coast would be affected. The BPRI had gained prominence and became a significant resource for Canadian and U.S. media as well as governments.

Forty-Year Milestone

The year 2011 marked 40 years since the formation of a formal Canadian–American Studies Program at Western. Mindful of the recent budget cuts and feeling some worry about the programs' future, Canadian Studies leaders decided to organize a gala celebration dinner to be followed by an academic conference. Our thinking was that an event of this kind would be a fitting way to celebrate the 40-year history of Canadian–American Studies, shine a spotlight on the extraordinary ties between the two countries, and gather researchers and political leaders to exchange ideas about prominent issues in Canada–U.S. relations. A wide-ranging audience was targeted, including the Western community—students, faculty, staff—and friends and supporters from the region, across the country, and throughout Canada.

The projected budget for the two-day event was in excess of $40,000. Funding came from ticket sales for the dinner and contributions from governments and businesses. Twenty-one companies from B.C. and Washington stepped up to help finance the events. Government support came from the Government of Canada, the Government of Alberta, and the Government of Québec. Other funding was received from the Port of Bellingham, the Canadian Studies Center at the University of Washington, the Pacific Northwest Economic Region, the White Rock/South Surrey B.C. Chamber of Commerce, the Pacific Corridor Enterprise Council, and the Cascadia Center for Regional Development. Many individuals and organizations purchased tables for 10 at $800 per table. A $10,000 grant from the Canadian government's Canadian Studies grants program supported the academic conference.

The planning for the 40th Anniversary events was assisted by several supporters from the Bellingham community: Jim Pettinger, President of International Market Access, a Ferndale, Washington, company that provides U.S.-based warehouse and business services for Canadian firms; Greg Boos, an immigration lawyer at Cascadia Cross Border Law, a Bellingham law firm specializing in Canadian immigration services; and Craig Cole, former owner of Brown and Cole, a grocery chain with a large store in Blaine, Washington, located less than a half mile from the border. All three were long-time friends of Canadian–American Studies and each had given a good deal of time and financial support to the program over the years. This group formed the core of the 40th Anniversary planning committee which also included Outreach Director Tina Storer, Program Manager Chuck Hart and graduate student and conference coordinator, Elliott Smith. The committee worked diligently, meeting almost weekly during an eight-month period prior to the event. All of us believed the 40th Anniversary events should make a statement about the importance of Canadian–American Studies to the campus, the Bellingham community, the region, and the state, and get the business community motivated to fully appreciate this fact. Just as important was demonstrating to university administrators the high regard in which Canadian Studies programs were held by people beyond the campus.

Two quite different events were organized with overlapping audiences on two consecutive days. The celebratory dinner was conceived as just that—a fun-filled evening of celebration involving a diverse group of people drawn primarily from Northwest Washington and the greater Vancouver, B.C., area. The conference on Canada–U.S. relations the following day featured prominent academics and policy officials from both countries.

Two high profile political figures—U.S. Ambassador to Canada David Jacobson and former Premier of Ontario Bob Rae—had accepted invitations to speak at both the dinner and conference, but both ended up canceling because a Canadian federal election was called for May 2, only three days after the 40th Anniversary events. The organizing committee scrambled to find substitutes—Phillip Chicola, United States Consul General of Canada, based in Vancouver, pinch hit for the ambassador, and David Emerson, a former Canadian federal cabinet minister, replaced Rae. Ambassador Jacobson agreed to send a video message in which he apologized for not being there in person: "When your boss is the President of the United States, and he asks you to do something, you do it."

The 40th Anniversary dinner was held on April 28th in the ballroom of the Hotel Bellwether situated on the Bellingham Bay waterfront. Western President Bruce Shepard led the speeches by commenting on the still-dire condition of the state budget. After painting a bleak picture of Western's finances and making everyone wonder if he was using the occasion to announce still more cuts to

Canadian–American Studies—or worse—he then, perhaps being more attuned to the occasion, shifted gears and talked about the Canadian programs at Western as assets to the university and the state. Governor Christine Gregoire sent a letter offering congratulations on "this exciting milestone" to the Canadian–American Studies program, followed by pointed observations about the importance of what was happening at Western:

> This Center is one of the oldest and prestigious Canadian Studies programs in the U.S., and it is the only one to have a research institute like the BPRI, which was created in 2005. Washington State and Canada enjoy a strong and fruitful friendship. We share a coast and a border, but more importantly, we share values—of innovation, integrity, collaboration and stewardship. I applaud the Center for its ongoing work to help us better understand our neighbors to the north, as well as promote research and dialogue on issues of mutual interest.[2]

As if taking a cue from the governor, the keynote, given by Chicola, highlighted the interconnectedness between the governments of B.C. and Washington state and the important role of Canadian programs at Western in strengthening bilateral relations. He commended the university for its long-time focus on Canada and particularly the work of the BPRI for providing data-driven research useful for policymakers in both countries. Chicola told the audience that the Cascadia region was known as the place where innovation in cross-border relations happens and Canadian programs at Western were pivotal in making this so.

Capping off the evening, following a dinner featuring West Coast salmon—perhaps from both B.C. and Washington depending on its migration route—and a presentation of an impressive 40th Anniversary cake in the shape of the Peace Arch, was a rousing musical performance by La Famille Leger, an Acadian music group with family roots in New Brunswick and Québec. The festive mood of the occasion fit our purpose of bringing the university and community together to celebrate the work and achievements of the 40-year-old program and pay tribute to the close personal relationships between the two countries.

Based on the number and variety of people in attendance, the 40th Anniversary dinner turned out to be highly successful. Tickets sold topped 300, exceeding expectations. The event raised funds for the creation of a 40th Anniversary Student Scholarship. Especially gratifying was the large number of people in attendance from outside the university and outside the state. Many were from Canada, showing that Canadian–American Studies at Western had become known and appreciated on both sides of the border.

On April 29, the day after the dinner, an all-day conference on Canadian–American relations was held. The conference, titled "Bridging Distances: Past and Future Perspectives on Canada–U.S. Relations," was intended as an exploration by scholars and diplomats of cross-border issues, including border management, energy policy, environment and trade. With border issues still front and center, conference participants offered views on possible scenarios for the future of Canada–U.S. relations. Much discussion centered on the role of states and provinces, local governments and region-based advocacy groups in finding ways to decrease the delays and bad experiences associated with crossing the border. One reporter at the conference observed:

> The Cascadia region is held up as a model of cooperation that others across the continent would do well to emulate. Numerous [conference] speakers singled out the Pacific Northwest Economic Region, the Whatcom Council of Governments, local efforts to become the first state and province to offer the enhanced driver's license, and other grass roots cooperation as examples of how to develop systems that work.[3]

A different take on the border was given by conference participant Elizabeth Jameson, a University of Calgary historian who had resided in both countries. Her paper, subtitled "Both Sides Now"—the title derived from the classic song written by Canadian recording artist Joni Mitchell—discussed how people perceive the 49th parallel in ways that relate to their own experience and the historical moments in which they live. Moving the conference discussion away from the rhetoric and actions of governments, and their almost singular focus on border security, Jameson said that before we can bridge distances between Canada and the U.S., both sides need to respectfully understand our different histories and be willing to confront distorted images of the neighboring country. "This history, like that of any good relationship," Jameson told the gathering,

> demands that we simultaneously recognize all that we share, while at the same time honoring our separate identities and respecting our boundaries. Twelve years of viewing our borders from both sides has convinced me that we need histories that cross our borders and link our pasts without erasing our differences. We cannot build relationships with people we cannot see across a boundary. We cannot build bridges across unmapped divides.[4]

Jameson was expressing a theme that has always been central to the mission of Canadian–American Studies at Western. The relationship between Canada and the United States involves—indeed centers on—daily cross-border connections among people. This human interaction, whether for personal reasons or economic opportunity, has always been the most crucial factor in maintaining harmonious relations between the two North American neighbors. As Jameson said, it is through human interaction that we see *across* the boundary. This is too often forgotten when border tensions dominate our perceptions and ultimately our understandings of one another.

The 40th Anniversary events were important in deepening the Center's bonds with its communities—both on and off campus—while reflecting on the Canadian programs' accomplishments and purpose. It seemed especially appropriate that on the occasion of celebrating 40 years of Canadian–American Studies at Western, the audiences were reminded that the border has always been more a space of connection than a point of division.

Lifting a Cloud of Uncertainty

In the fall of 2012, Western Provost Catherine Riordan appointed a group of faculty and staff to form a task force to "host strategic conversations regarding the future of the Canadian–American Studies Program and the Border Policy Research Institute." Riordan stated the purpose of the task force as follows:

> I charge the task force to work with internal and external constituencies, experts, and key stakeholders to recommend the most desirable future strategic directions and organizational location of the Center for Canadian–American Studies and the Border Policy Research Institute. by December 1, 2012.[5]

I suspected the provost's underlying purpose was to get validation for downsizing the programs, along with consensus for reorganizing Canadian Studies. My suspicion was not allayed by Riordan's statement about why she formed the task force. She wrote:

> A number of internal and external issues and circumstances are the impetus for this task force. Internally, the university has developed a new mission statement. Unprecedented budget cuts have forced a closer look at all academic programs particularly those outside traditional "core" instruction. The Center for International Studies is in transition, and issues of organizational structure and succession in Canadian–American Studies and BPRI are under study.[6]

There was no specific charge to recommend budget cuts, although the task force was pointedly told that the university's financial problems had forced greater scrutiny of non-core academic programs. Riordan's instruction to the committee included consideration of future re-organization possibilities, new sources of funding from off campus, as well as growth opportunities for Canadian Studies.

Joe Garcia, a professor of management in the College of Business and Economics and head of the university's Bowman Leadership Program, was appointed chair of the task force. The other seven members included two deans, the vice president for external relations, and four faculty from economics, political science, environmental studies, and the Western library. Task force members, about half with Canadian Studies ties, were assigned the job of interviewing faculty, students and several persons off campus who had connections with the program. Twenty-one individuals, chosen from private, educational, government and nonprofit sectors, as well as alumni of the two programs, were interviewed. The interviewees consisted of both Canadians and Americans. Based on the interviews, the task force was charged with issuing a final report with recommendations.

The completed work of the task force was compiled in a report, "Canadian–American Studies/Border Policy Research Institute Task Force Recommendation," dated December 2012. The report did not propose any new budget cuts for Canadian–American Studies or the BPRI. In fact, the report recommended that the university "invest in and develop greater capacity to market and fund both entities [referring to Can-Am Studies and the BPRI]."[7] The report acknowledged that shrunken state and federal budgets made future government funding more problematic and urged the Canadian programs to focus more on private sector organizations that had a direct interest in, or benefited from, Canadian Studies entities at Western. Comments from the stakeholders who contributed to the report discussed several funding ideas, including a stronger focus on the policy and business communities, new partnerships with other universities (in Canada and the U.S.) who were doing similar work, and a more systematic effort to enlist support from local and national foundations. The report, also pointed to the need for the university's fundraising arm—the Western Foundation—to lend more assistance to the Canadian Studies' programs in their efforts to seek new donors.

On the question of where organizationally the Canadian programs belonged in the overall structure of Western, the task force members overwhelmingly favored keeping the programs outside of academic departments and independent from the Center for International Studies (CIS). As discussed throughout this book, over the years Western's administrators were of several minds about where Canadian programs fit in the overall college structure, and to whom (dean, provost, or some other administrator) they should report. In the early years, Canadian–American Studies reported to the dean of the College of Arts and Sciences. Finding this unsatisfactory because Canadian–American Studies had faculty participants in most of the colleges across the university, the line of reportage was changed to come under the provost. In theory this made sense because provosts were responsible for overseeing all the university's academic programs. A problem with this arrangement was that the needs of a relatively small, interdepartmental program simply got lost within the political give-and-take of the provost's office where allocating resources to all academic departments was handled.

So, this begged the question: Should the Canadian programs, obviously international in nature, be placed under international studies? The Center for International Studies at Western was an umbrella organization that oversaw an international studies minor, administered study-abroad programs, and organized speaker events on campus. But it was unclear to me—and as it turned out, to task force members—how being part of CIS could add value to Canadian–American Studies. CIS was not like the Henry M. Jackson School of International Studies at the University of Washington, headed by a dean, and the home of several well-funded area studies programs, including the UW Center for Canadian Studies.

The idea of moving Canadian programs into CIS did not sit well with many, if not most, of the task force members. One respondent remarked that, "Including Can-Am/BPRI in international studies would risk burying the brand and eventually lose the focus and unique niche that the programs serve." Another said, "I'm wary of including Can-Am in the Center for International Studies because it has the potential of getting lost in a larger unit."[8] Concern was expressed about whether the Canada programs could continue to be a significant force in Canada–U.S. relations if they were part of a broader bureaucratic structure. One task force respondent said:

> I fear integration [with the Center for International Studies] might increase the possibility of leading decision makers for the program not really having a pulse on the U.S.–Canada relationship or the special issues surrounding it. I accept there may be other benefits for efficiency, but I would tread very carefully.[9]

In its final report, the task force recommended that the current organizational structure of Canadian Studies programs remain unchanged: "Maintain the existing structure, with the Canadian–American Studies Program continuing to report to the Provost and the Border Policy Research Institute continuing to report to the Vice Provost for Research."[10]

Another organizational question was whether Canadian–American Studies and the BPRI should be combined into one unit. None of the interviewees supported such a merger. The two entities, although closely aligned in their function of providing knowledge of Canada and Canada–U.S. relations, had different purposes and audiences. One interviewee observed that the two entities were engaged in "synergistic interaction between applied research as conducted by [the] BPRI [using] faculty and graduate students, and the undergraduate-focused academic programs exemplified by the Can-Am program."[11]

In its final report, the task force rejected merging the two programs with this explanation: "While interviewees understood the economic exigencies of the institution, none of the respondents volunteered merging the two entities or incorporating them into other units, as they have two distinct functions."[12]

Overall, the Task Force Recommendation turned out to be a strong reaffirmation of the value of the Canadian programs at Western. Canadian–American Studies and BPRI activities were viewed as satisfying important needs for education, government and business on both sides of the border. As mentioned several times in the task force report, few universities were educating students about Canada and Canada–U.S. relations and, to quote one of the interviewed persons, "there isn't anybody else who is doing the important work that the BPRI engages in."[13] It is worth quoting a key line in the report's Executive Summary:

> One theme is superordinate to the specific recommendations: both the Canadian–American Studies Program and the Border Policy Research Institute are, as one interviewee said, crown jewels for the university as they offer distinctive value to an important and unique community that is not duplicated.[14]

The Task Force Recommendation, released December 2012, was not a roadmap for retrenchment or organizational change for Canadian programs. The existing structure with Canadian–American Studies reporting to the provost and the BPRI reporting to the vice provost for research was thought to be sound, or at least a better choice than the alternatives. The Canadian–American Studies mission of providing educational services and resources focused on Canada, and the BPRI's mission of engaging in applied research primarily focused on the Pacific Northwest region, but with an eye open to other research opportunities further afield, was not disputed. As for funding, the Canadian programs were urged to seek project grants and explore partnerships with private sector organizations and universities in Canada. These avenues had been, and would continue to be, pursued.

It is not known what the provost might have expected, or hoped for, by establishing the task force. Most likely she was looking for ideas on how to create cost efficiencies. She probably was anticipating a recommendation to consolidate the programs under international studies or perhaps in one of the academic departments. Fortunately, as I saw it, the task force recommended a different outcome.

From my vantage point as director of Canadian–American Studies and the BPRI, the Task Force Recommendation turned out to be important in lifting a cloud of uncertainty about the future of Canadian Studies in light of the budget cuts a few years earlier. Perhaps most important, the task force exercise served to legitimize the value of Canadian Studies programs to Western and to off-campus constituencies, as well as indicate where opportunity might lie for the future.

Salish Sea Institute

The Center for Canadian–American Studies and the Border Policy Research Institute offered models of how Western could continue to develop border-related programs that contribute to the university and its mission. Western, located in the heart of the border-spanning Salish Sea ecosystem, was well situated by geography and expertise to develop an interdepartmental program to study the changes occurring in the inland sea resulting from rapid economic and population growth in the surrounding urban region. The university, through its biology department, Huxley College of the Environment, and the Shannon Point Marine Center (located in Anacortes, Washington), had a great deal of expertise in the science and ecology of the Salish Sea—the name given in 2010 to the cross-border inland marine waters encompassing the Strait of Georgia in British Columbia and the Puget Sound and Strait of Juan de Fuca in Washington state. Already much academic work was being done on different aspects of the Salish Sea, and interest among students, faculty and community groups was growing. What wasn't being done was approaching the ecosystem as one international body. The time was right for creating an umbrella center or institute with a mission of studying and advancing responsible stewardship of the Salish Sea as a singular, cross-border ecosystem.

In the fall of 2012, Canadian–American Studies hosted a meeting of scientists, government officials and NGOs from both sides of the border to explore how to improve cooperation among B.C. and Washington state scientists working on Salish Sea issues. The meeting was held under the auspices of the Puget Sound Partnership (PSP), a Washington state agency responsible for coordinating actions to restore and protect the Puget Sound—the part of the Salish Sea south of the 49th parallel. The meeting in Bellingham, surprisingly, was the first time the PSP directly involved its Canadian counterparts. At the end of the day's deliberations, in a free-wheeling discussion of "next steps," some of the participants raised the idea of a distinguished professorship of Salish Sea Studies that would rotate between universities in Washington and British Columbia. One of the anticipated responsibilities of the professorship would be to organize the Salish Sea Ecosystem Conference (SSEC), a large gathering held every two years, alternating between Seattle and Vancouver, B.C., that in some years drew upwards of a thousand researchers and government and tribal/First Nations leaders from both Canada and the United States. Although the distinguished professorship idea was ultimately rejected as too farfetched, the SSEC was much on the minds of people at the meeting because the future of the conference was uncertain.

Since 2003, the SSEC had been organized under the aegis of the Canadian and U.S. federal environment departments—Environment Canada and the Environmental Protection Agency—with Washington state and B.C. environmental departments also playing key roles. After the 2011 Salish Sea Ecosystem Conference, both federal governments, mostly for financial reasons, decided not to underwrite the event in future years and thus what had become the premier cross-border environmental event in the region was in danger of ending unless a new sponsoring entity could be found. Seeing this as an opportunity for the Center and the university, I made it known during a reception at Canada House for the cross-border science meeting, that Canadian–American Studies would be interested in serving as the organizing body for the next SSEC conference. My offer was enthusiastically supported by Wayne Landis, the Director of Western's Institute for Environmental Toxicology and a professor at Huxley College. Landis had been closely involved with the SSEC for many years, served as a member of the Puget Sound Partnership, always a main player in the conference, and had good contacts with the British Columbia marine science community. Though my offer was only that, it was evident to me that those at the Bellingham science meeting, most of whom were active in past Salish Sea Ecosystem Conferences, were interested in having Western take over the administrative responsibility of running an SSEC in 2014. Of course, for the offer to be achievable, the university would have to commit to it and this would require upfront monetary assurances.

Getting Western's administrators to support the conference

required the help of allies outside of Canadian–American Studies. One key supporter was Steve Hollenhorst, the recently hired dean of Huxley College, who became a champion of the idea of Western taking charge of the conference. Hollenhorst was instrumental in getting the provost to agree to commit seed money to support conference planning and preparation. With this commitment, Canadian–American Studies, on behalf of Western, submitted a proposal outlining why the university was interested in the SSEC, which entities would be involved, and what resources would be made available. While the provost would put up most of the planning money, the Center would provide the administrative staff work. Western's proposal was accepted by an ad hoc SSEC executive committee made up of persons who were leaders in previous conferences. Agreement was reached that the SSEC would be held in Seattle in May of 2014.

As the lead administrative unit (secretariat) for the 2014 SSEC in Seattle, the Center for Canadian–American Studies hired a conference administrator, and assumed responsibility for all budget actions pertaining to the event. An executive committee consisting of scientists and persons from NGOs in Washington state and British Columbia, shaped the program and lined up potential donors. Initial funding from the provost covered basic administrative costs, including supporting a significant fund-raising campaign. Assuming grants and donations could be secured in an amount roughly equal to what was raised for the 2011 meeting, and registrations would at least meet—and hopefully exceed—previous SSEC participation levels, we expected the large meeting to pay for itself and possibly turn a profit.

The yearlong organizing effort for the conference overwhelmed the small, understaffed Center, but the final product was worth it. The Salish Sea Ecosystem Conference held April 30–May 2, 2014, at the Washington State Convention Center in Seattle turned out to be the largest ever. More than 1,200 registrations were received. Donations from sponsors exceeded what was received for the 2011 meeting. When revenue from registrations was added to the sponsorships, the result was a profit of just under $100,000. It was not lost on Western's administrators that the success of the 2014 conference was in no small part due to the work of the Center, aided by Wayne Landis and his Huxley College colleagues and the committed staff at Western's Conference Services office. The profit made by the 2014 SSEC was seen by the provost as a nice plum that could help fund future Salish Sea projects.

While there was already interest in creating a formal Salish Sea program on campus, the successful 2014 Salish Sea Ecosystem Conference provided momentum to galvanize action. One individual who was a longtime proponent of establishing a Salish Sea studies program at the university was Bert Webber, a retired marine biology professor at Huxley College and the person who more than anyone else was responsible for building support to get the awkward three-part name of the inland waters—Puget Sound-Strait of Georgia-Strait of Juan de Fuca—changed to the singular and more culturally fitting designation, Salish Sea. Webber believed the name change was especially important for scientists trying to study an ecosystem holistically that spans two nations. As he was fond of saying, "you can't know something that doesn't have a name." Webber spent the better part of two decades in a quest to convince federal, state and provincial bodies to approve the more geographically and culturally correct name. He was finally successful in 2009 when government agencies in the U.S. formally approved use of the name Salish Sea and authorized its use on maps, with the same name change occurring in Canada the following year.

Western Associate Provost Brian Burton, who in 2013 had been given responsibility for overseeing interdisciplinary programs on campus and was now the person to whom Canadian–American Studies reported, became a strong proponent of a new, still undefined, academic institute that would encompass Salish Sea studies. Huxley College Dean Steve Hollenhorst attended the 2014 conference in Seattle, and came home excited about leveraging the event into something lasting and permanent on the Western campus.

Impressed with the success of the 2014 SSEC, Burton, soon after the conference, convened a planning committee composed of faculty and administrators to begin consideration of a standalone

Salish Sea program at Western. A major consideration for Burton, and shared by everyone on the planning committee, was to ensure that whatever was created involved a significant partnership with the Northwest Indian College located on the Lummi Reservation a few miles west of Bellingham. It was unimaginable to the planning committee that a program focused on the Salish Sea could succeed without the participation of Coast Salish peoples. The Northwest Indian College was prominent for its academic programs serving Indigenous populations and the college featured a well-developed marine science program and growing Salish Sea research institute. Most importantly, Western is situated on the ancestral homelands of the Coast Salish peoples who have lived in the area since time immemorial.

The deliberations about a Salish Sea program ran for several months. Throughout the process, Burton was unequivocal about his commitment to the project and this proved vital to its eventual realization. By the summer of 2015, the various university committees had given their assent to the creation of a Salish Sea Studies Institute (later shortened to Salish Sea Institute) at Western. The institute would focus on teaching and public outreach aimed at making students and the community more aware of what is needed individually and collectively to restore and preserve the Salish Sea. Webber put it this way:

> Residents of the Salish Sea region acknowledge there are issues about it that need to be addressed ... to give a voice to those concerns, there needs to be cross-boundary organizations and outreach, and that this is the interesting and beneficial aspects of the [Salish Sea] Institute—to foster those relationships and stewardships.[15]

The Salish Sea Institute was officially launched in fall of 2015 with Bert Webber appointed as its interim director. His knowledge of the Salish Sea, scientific connections on both sides of the border and association with the Salish Sea name change made him a natural choice to be the founding director to launch the institute during its start-up phase. Webber was action oriented and hoped the institute could be a catalyst for the B.C. and Washington governments to commit to a serious cross-border problem solving agenda—which could include a treaty or international compact—for addressing the deteriorating condition of the Salish Sea ecosystem. Having already retired, Webber served for an interim period of eighteen months at the end of which Ginny Broadhurst was appointed to be the institute's first permanent director in June 2017.

Broadhurst, not an academic by background, brought an "in the trenches" approach to the work of the institute. In previous jobs, particularly in her role as executive director of the Northwest Straits Commission—an organization closely associated with tribes, First Nations, and environmental groups on both sides of the border—she was adept at creating and communicating practical solutions to environmental problems. Her scientific credentials were solid having earned a master's degree from the School of Marine Affairs at the University of Washington. A person with extensive knowledge of marine science and effective public outreach skills, Broadhurst saw her job as creating a bridge between the scientific community, policy officials and the people who inhabit the Salish Sea.

The Salish Sea Institute's core mission—"to foster responsible stewardship in our ecosystem, inspiring and informing its protection for the benefit of current and future generations"—allowed for a great deal of leeway in setting the direction of the institute. This was by intention as the people involved in the organization's creation were not of one mind about what it would be in practice. There was, however, general agreement that the institute would offer an interdisciplinary curriculum in Salish Sea Studies and be a credible educational voice for informing the public about the importance of, and perils facing, the Salish Sea ecosystem.

By 2019, the programmatic contours of the institute became clear. A minor in Salish Sea studies was in place with emphasis on the ecologies and human experiences of the ecosystem as well as transboundary governance relationships and tribal sovereignty. In partnership with Huxley College, an annual speaker series was developed. The institute became the administrative home of the

Salish Sea Ecosystem Conference. Public outreach to community groups, schools and political leaders was ongoing. The Salish Sea Institute was now, like the Border Policy Research Institute and Center for Canadian–American Studies, an integral component of Canadian Studies at Western.

Into the Future

I retired on December 31, 2014, forty-three years and four months after I was first appointed to a one-year position in the political science department in 1971. Canadian Studies had become a passion and I never tired of trying to educate Americans about the importance of our neighbors.

I watched Canadian–American Studies at Western grow from a small program to a large multidisciplinary Center housing three distinct but highly complementary programs—Center for Canadian–American Studies, the Border Policy Research Institute, and the recently formed Salish Sea Institute—with faculty and staff involved from across the reach of the university. In combination, Canadian Studies programs at Western formed one of the strongest of its kind in North America, and with new commitment from the university and program leaders, the future looked bright.

I was pleased to have played a role in the appointment of two successors: David Rossiter, who assumed the directorship of the Center in the fall of 2014, and Laurie Trautman, hired in 2014 as associate director of the BPRI and later appointed director in 2016. In 2015, my decade-long colleague David Davidson returned to the institute to serve as BPRI interim director for one year to manage the transition following my retirement.

Rossiter embarked on a major restructuring of the Canadian–American Studies curriculum so that it would better meet the needs of students and reflect the growing importance of cultural and environmental issues in Canada and throughout North America. He successfully piloted two innovative Title VI grant proposals, marking thirty consecutive years of success in obtaining Department of Education grant funding, in partnership with the Canadian Studies

Center at the University of Washington. Also, during Rossiter's term as director, discussions began with the university administration about hiring a tenure track professor in Canadian–American Studies, certainly a major step forward for the academic program.

Trautman's stewardship of the BPRI has been just as impressive. An expanded partnership with the University of Victoria led to new research opportunities as well as a joint University of Victoria–Western border fellows program that has attracted border scholars from around the world. Fieldwork at the Cascadia border crossings, always utilizing Western students, continued to be expanded, and outreach to policy leaders reached a new level. A three-way partnership with the University of Windsor Cross-Border Institute and the University at Buffalo–State University of New York was formed to publish an updated "Border Barometer" that highlights performance metrics at each border crossing in terms of the movement of people and goods. With the COVID pandemic crisis in 2020, the BPRI became a vital source of information about the impacts of the closure of the border and how border security suddenly became intertwined with public health issues.

Following a four-year term as Center director, Rossiter elected to step down and return full-time to the geography program in Huxley College.

In the fall of 2018, Christina Keppie, associate professor of French and Linguistics in the Modern and Classical Languages department, was appointed director of the Center. Keppie at the time of her appointment was editor of the journal, *The American Review of Canadian Studies*, a position she held since May 2015. Among her teaching accomplishments was a popular summer program that took Western students to Québec in association with the University of Québec at Montreal to study French. Keppie, who has roots in the Acadian part of New Brunswick, received her doctorate in French Language, Literature and Linguistics from the University of Alberta. She specializes in the culture of the Acadian diaspora throughout the Canadian Maritime provinces, Québec and Maine, thereby bringing an important, but often neglected, aspect of

Francophone Canada to the Canadian–American Studies academic program.

I was not privy to the discussions leading to the renovation and reorganization of Canada House that began only months following my retirement. Needless to say, when I learned of carpenters and painters in the building, I was more than pleased. However it happened, the renovations that were made to the building fulfilled a decades-long objective held by many of us of saving the house and combining all the Canadian programs at Western in one place. The downstairs kitchen was converted into a well-appointed office for the program manager. The dining room was modified to provide multiple work stations for staff. The glassed-in front room that looked out on Bellingham Bay and Canada in the distance was remodeled to make it more functional space for conducting small classes and meetings. My old upstairs office, which in my opinion has the best view of any workplace on campus, became the office of the director of the Salish Sea Institute. The other upstairs room facing the bay was assigned to the director of the BPRI. The office for the director of the Center for Canadian–American Studies was moved downstairs to the fireplace room, once the formal living room when the house was a private residence. The reconfigured space maximized the potential of the house as the academic home of expanding Canadian Studies activities at Western.

Canada House was officially the home of what was now called Canada House Programs, bringing together in one building the newly formed Salish Sea Institute, the Border Policy Research Institute and the Center for Canadian–American Studies. The three directors of these programs shared staff and worked in close proximity, an arrangement intended to encourage more collaboration and better communication.

Tina Storer retired as director of K–12 outreach in 2016 and Kyla Sweet, a native of Alberta who is bilingual, was named K–12 Education and Curriculum Specialist in 2018. In the new configuration, Chuck Hart remained the program manager for the Center until he retired in April 2020 and Ruth Musonda was hired as program assistant for all three programs. A new position, Associate Director of Transboundary Initiatives, was created to provide research, grant writing and public outreach support for the Center and the affiliated institutes. Natalie J.K. Baloy, who holds a Ph.D. in cultural anthropology from the University of British Columbia was appointed to this role. Baloy also teaches courses in Salish Sea Studies. Following Chuck Hart's retirement, Lisl Schroeder became the Canadian–American Studies program coordinator in May 2020.

The deliberations about creating a tenure-track position in Canadian–American Studies, begun by David Rossiter, finally bore fruit. In fact, the effort was so successful that in 2019, two tenure-track positions were created. Both positions, based in Canadian–American Studies, focused on comparative Indigenous studies signaling the importance to which the university had come to regard this area. The positions are joint appointments in Canadian–American Studies and the Salish Sea Institute, as well as in the academic departments of the faculty members' area of specialization. As Canadian Studies at Western passes the half-century mark in 2021, the personnel and resources are firmly in place to assure future success.

Conclusion

This book began by showing how a handful of faculty at Western Washington State College—now Western Washington University—embarked on a journey to create a program for the study of Canada. Only a few such programs existed in the United States and none were in the western part of the country. So, why then did a Canadian–American Studies program take root at what was historically a teachers college located in the remote northwest corner of Washington state? Part of the answer lies in geography and the resulting economic, social, and ecological relationships it begets. Canada is next door, and because of the north-south orientation of mountains and watersheds and historic cross-border flows of people and commerce, the presence of Canada is an inexorable force of influence in this part of Washington.

The border marks a political divide, but it also acts as a gateway for reciprocal social and economic relationships. Bellingham and Western are located in a borderland region where just the existence of an international border affects traffic volumes, retail business, criminal activity, real estate values and policing and security. In this setting, to ignore Canada would be all but impossible. For our educational system to overlook the Canadian presence would be like disregarding a part of the place in which we live.

Interest in developing Canadian Studies programs at Western was also prompted by worries from academics and community leaders that Canada–U.S. relations was moving into a more contentious phase. As discussed throughout this book, Canada and the U.S. often have had policy differences on issues of common concern.

In the 1970s, the British Columbia government's pricing of natural gas exported to the United States was viewed by many Americans as capricious, resulting in tensions in cross-border relations. Over the years, Canadian and U.S. fishers have clashed over salmon harvests leading to difficult bargaining to achieve outcomes acceptable to both countries. Since 9/11, heavy-handed U.S. security policies at the border have irritated Canadians because they have slowed commerce and added costs to exports bound for the U.S.

More recently, the tariffs put on Canada during the Trump administration soured the relationship further, leading to retaliatory actions by Canada, and threatened to embroil both nations in an all-out trade war. In 2020, the COVID-19 pandemic led to a border shutdown of all nonessential cross-border travel. Canadian and U.S. differences in the levels of infection and dissimilar approaches for dealing with the virus likely will complicate border crossings and strain relationships for some time to come.

From the beginning, the work of the Center for Canadian–American Studies has been influenced by worries that misunderstandings and poorly conceived policies could undermine the harmony and goodwill that has been a hallmark of the relationship. The landmark Canadian–American Symposium held in 1974 was an early project aimed at bringing Canadian and U.S. policymakers together to better understand issues and the views held by counterparts on the other side of the border. That symposium was the beginning of many events at Western aimed at educating students, the public and policymakers about Canada.

Since the beginning of a formal Canadian–American Studies Program in 1971, the Center's teaching and public outreach has focused, in one way or another, on creating informed citizens and public officials. This has challenged Canadian–American Studies to provide objective information and practical knowledge, without

Conclusion

serving the agendas of any government or interest group. Put another way, academics must avoid surrendering their independence to become propagandists for authority. This can be a difficult balancing act, especially when a good deal of Canadian Studies funding has come from the U.S. and Canadian governments. It is worth noting that in my experience government grants have never come with pressure to follow a particular course of action. Canadian Studies leaders and supporting politicians have properly recognized that teaching and research must remain independent from political agendas. The Center has never viewed itself as a training school for diplomats, nor should it. Canadian Studies aims to prepare people to be contributing citizens and public intellectuals who are mindful and respectful about Canada and other societies to which Americans are intricately connected.

A certain amount of idealism has influenced Canadian Studies programs at Western. President Franklin D. Roosevelt once said that "we are so accustomed to an undefended boundary three thousand [sic] miles long that we are inclined perhaps to minimize its vast importance, not only to our own continuing relations but also to the example which it sets to the other nations of the world." In my own teaching, I have urged students to think about how the history of harmonious interactions across the Canadian–American border, and particularly the close cross-border relations that have developed in the Cascadia corner of North America, should be—as Roosevelt believed—a model for emulation across the globe.

There would be no Canadian Studies programs at Western without the commitment and dedication of individual faculty, staff and supportive administrators. As this book has shown, moving the concept of Canadian Studies from an idea to actuality was not an easy task. Unlike traditional university programs rooted in the liberal arts and science disciplines, Canadian Studies had to be pretty much invented from the ground up. Fortunately, resourceful and forward-looking faculty such as Barry Gough, James Scott, Gerard Rutan and Robert Monahan had the foresight and determination to push boundaries of conventional academic practice to advance new ideas for programs that crossed departments and colleges. Skepticism that such programs could succeed was rampant, money was in short supply, and Western's faculty were burdened by heavy teaching loads. Nonetheless, entrepreneurial leaders found ways to make a fledgling Canadian–American Studies Program work. The term "bootstrapping" was commonly used to describe the work of remarkably self-sufficient pioneers like Rutan and Monahan. Considering that Canadian–American Studies did not have an office of its own for the first six years of its existence, nor a dedicated secretary, nor even release time for the director, it is a wonder there was a program at all.

Canadian–American Studies was always a hybrid between a traditional academic program in a disciplinary department and a thinktank-like body focused on producing knowledge to assist citizens in professional roles to better deal with cross-border problems and take advantage of regional opportunities. For this reason, Canadian–American Studies continually wrestled with finding its place in the Western collegiate structure. In many ways, the programs were, and still are, orphans in an institution that frankly did not quite know what to do with them. Yet, few at the university or in the community ever questioned the value of programs focused on educating Americans about Canada and its web of relationships with the United States. To the contrary, as we have shown, a deep vein of support for Canadian–American Studies has been present on the Western campus, in the surrounding community and conveyed by public officials, business groups and the media for more than a half century.

Much of the story of the history of Canadian Studies at Western is about how a small group of people over the years have embraced a widely felt need for a university-based program of education and public diplomacy dealing with Canada. The locus of this half-century project is Canada House, which sits like an observatory on Sehome Hill, looking northward across Bellingham

Bay gazing, not at the stars, but at Canada on the horizon. Like an observatory, Canada House is a place for scientific study of a neighboring society, that is observable, accessible, and researchable. Canada house, like an observatory, provides an institutional capability for organizing a wide range of knowledge and skills beyond what a single researcher or department could manage. Just as important, Canada House, with its flagstaff flying both American and Canadian flags, is an impressive symbol of respect, comity and pride with which Western, Bellingham, and the State of Washington regard our northern neighbor.

Chapter Notes

Chapter 1: The Setting

1. Cited in Flora, C. J. *Normal College Knowledge: A Sometimes Humorous, Sometimes Sad, but Always Loving Inside View of Western*, Everson, WA: JERO (1991) 101.

2. Kremen, Jill. "Legion—Students Explode," *Western Front* (October 30, 1970).

3. Bryan, M. L. Jr. "The College of Ethnic Studies at Western Washington University: A Case Study." Masters Thesis, WWU Graduate School Collection, 825 (1993) 91.

4. Cited in the Alumni Newsletter—*Resumé*, Volume 18, No. 4 (January, 1977).

Chapter 2: Beginnings

1. Letter from R. Kaiser to H. Bunke, December 8, 1965, Records of President's Office, Box 3, University Archives, Western Washington University, Accession No. 83-23.

2. Letter from R. Kaiser to H. Bunke, December 8, 1965, Records of President's Office, Box 3, University Archives, Western Washington University, Accession No. 83-23.

3. Letter from B. Goltz to R. Kaiser, March 3, 1966, Records of President's Office, Box 3, University Archives, Western Washington University, Accession No. 83-23.

4. Letter from H. Taylor to H. Bunke, August 8, 1966, Records of President's Office, Box 3, University Archives, Western Washington University, Accession No. 83-23.

5. Memo from B. Gough to J. Bumstead, July 16, 1970, Records of President's Office, Box 3, University Archives, Western Washington University, Accession No. 83-23.

6. Cited in *FAST* (a faculty and staff newsletter), Volume 2, No 32 (July, 1970).

7. Thomson, D. C. and R. F. Swanson. "Scholars, Missionaries or Counter-Imperialists?" *American Review of Canadian Studies*, 1:1 (1971) 2-13. This attitude about Canadians continued among some ACSUS leaders at least up to the time I retired in 2014. The mindset was that Canadian academics in the U.S. would try to dictate the direction of Canadian Studies in the United States.

8. Written Brief from B. Gough to D. Alper, "The Origins of Canadian Studies at Western Washington University: Some Recollections," 2019, Personal Correspondence held by D. Alper.

Chapter 3: Getting it on the Map

1. A discussion of Canadian Studies in the United States as an instrument of Canadian foreign policy is found in Brooks, S. *Promoting Canadian Studies Abroad: Soft Power and Cultural Diplomacy*, New York: Palgrave-Macmillan (2018).

2. Memo from J. Davis to R. Monahan, March 13, 1978, Records of President's Office, Box 3, University Archives, Western Washington University, Accession No. 83-23.

3. Quoted in Groen, J. P., "British Columbia's International Relations: Consolidating a Coalition Building Strategy," *B.C. Studies*, No. 102 (Summer 1974). The source of the quote is the *Vancouver Sun* (September 21, 1974) 1.

4. "Blue Eyed Arab Gas Plan Riles U.S." *The Columbian* (January 11, 1975) 1.

5. "Time to Sit Down Calmly," *Bellingham Herald* (September 18, 1974), Records of Communications and Marketing, Box 2, University Archives, Western Washington University, Accession No. 85-21.

6. "Can-Am Symposium—49th Parallel Blindness," *Skagit Valley Herald* (September 20, 1974), Records of Communications and Marketing, Box 2, University Archives, Western Washington University, Accession No. 85-21.

7. Rutan's comment is quoted from his testimony at a hearing on Canadian relations with the United States, at The Standing Senate Committee on Foreign Affairs, Government of Canada (March 13, 1975) 13:8.

8. "Historic Canadian-Washington Meeting Set," *Skagit Valley Herald* (July 9, 1974), Records of Communications and Marketing, Box 2, University Archives, Western Washington University, Accession No. 85-21.

9. "Meeds Urges Rational Talk on U.S.-Canadian Problems," *Bellingham Herald* (September 22, 1974), Records of Communication and Marketing, Box 2, University Archives, Western Washington University, Accession No. 85-21.

10. "Border Problems Talked at Only by Those at Symposium," *Bellingham Herald* (September 24, 1974), Records of Communication and Marketing, Box

2, University Archives, Western Washington University, Accession No. 85-21.

11. "Evans, Barrett Pledge Conservation, Little Else," *Bellingham Herald* (September 22, 1974), Records of Communication and Marketing, Box 2, University Archives, Western Washington University, Accession No. 85-21.

12. "Special Committee on Canadian Problems Urged," *Bellingham Herald* (September 25, 1974), Records of Communication and Marketing, Box 2, University Archives, Western Washington University, Accession No. 85-21.

13. The Government of British Columbia's thinking on setting up a formal structure with Washington State is discussed at a hearing on Canadian relations with the United States at The Standing Senate Committee on Foreign Affairs, Government of Canada (March 13, 1975) 13:12.

Chapter 4: A Flurry of Activity

1. Brucas III, Angelo. "Olscamp: Ambition Knows No Boundaries," *Klipsun Magazine*, Vol 8, No. 1 (November, 1977).

2. Memo from G. Rutan to Can-Am Program Faculty, February 4, 1976, Records of President's Office, Box 3, University Archives, Western Washington University, Accession No. 83-23.

3. Ibid.

4. Letter from G. Rutan to P. Olscamp, February 5, 1976, Records of President's Office, Box 3, University Archives, Western Washington University, Accession No. 83-23.

5. Letter from P. Olscamp to G. Rutan, February 17, 1976, Records of President's Office, Box 3, University Archives, Western Washington University, Accession No. 83-23.

6. Letter from P. Olscamp to R. Monahan, March 30, 1976, Records of President's Office, Box 3, University Archives, Western Washington University, Accession No. 83-23.

7. Memorandum from G. Rutan to Canadian–American Studies Faculty, May 3, 1976, Records of President's Office, Box 3, University Archives, Western Washington University, Accession No. 83-23.

8. Letter from R. Teshera to G. Rutan, May 6, 1976, Records of President's Office, Box 3, University Archives, Western Washington University, Accession No. 83-23.

9. Letter from P. Olscamp to J. Davis, July 9, 1976, Records of President's Office, Box 3, University Archives, Western Washington University, Accession No. 83-23.

10. Letter from L. Webb to P. Olscamp, June 18, 1976, Records of President's

Office, Box 3, University Archives, Western Washington University, Accession No. 83-23.

11. Minutes from the Canadian–American Studies Faculty Meeting, September 29, 1976, Records of President's Office, Box 3, University Archives, Western Washington University, Accession No. 83-23. Vernon's request to read his statement and Davis' response regarding emeritus faculty are all included in the minutes from the September 29 faculty meeting.

12. Minutes from the Canadian–American Studies Faculty Meeting, October 21, 1976, Records of President's Office, Box 3, University Archives, Accession No. 83-23.

13. September 1977-June 1978 Academic Planning Process document from R. Monahan, October 31, 1977, Records of President's Office, Box 5, University Archives, Western Washington University. Accession No. 83-23.

14. Ibid.

15. Ibid.

16. Letter from R. Monahan to P. Olscamp, April 12, 1977, Records of President's Office, Box 5, University Archives, Western Washington University, Accession No. 83-23.

17. Schwartz, J. "Canada House is Officially Dedicated," cited in the Alumni Newsletter—*Résumé*, Volume 10, No. 6 (March, 1979).

Chapter 5: Ebb and Flow

1. Speech transcript, January 22, 1980, Records of Communications and Marketing, Box 1, University Archives, Western Washington University, Accession No. 82-18.

2. September 1977-June 1978 Academic Planning Process document from Robert Monahan, October 31, 1977, Records of President's Office, Box 5, University Archives, Western Washington University, Accession No. 83-23.

3. Memo from J. Scott, March 13, 1978, Records of President's Office, Box 3, (Canadian–American Studies File 3), University Archives, Western Washington University, Accession No. 83-23.

4. Letter from P. Olscamp to J. Colthart, April 24, 1979, Records of President's Office, Box 3, (Canadian–American Studies File 2), University Archives, Western Washington University, Accession No. 83-23.

5. Letter from J. Davis to R. Monahan, October 22, 1979, Records of President's Office, Box 1, (Canadian–American Studies File 2), University Archives, Western Washington University, Accession No. 83-23.

6. Letter from R. Monahan to G. R. Ross, December 13 1982, Records of

Chapter Notes

President's Office, Box 6, (Canadian–American Studies File), University Archives, Western Washington University, Accession No. 85-25.

7. Letter from R. Monahan to P. Olscamp, February 25, 1981, Records of President's Office, Box 6, (Canadian–American Studies File), University Archives, Western Washington University, Accession No. 85-25.

8. Note from J. Talbot to G. R. Ross, pasted to Monahan to Ross letter, December 13 1982, Records of President's Office, Box 6, (Canadian–American Studies File), University Archives, Western Washington University, Accession No. 85-25.

9. Letter from R. Van Dyken to D. Alper, July 16, 1981, Canadian–American Studies Files, Canada House, Western Washington University.

10. Letter from W. Chance to W. G. Magnuson, May 14, 1980, Records of President's Office, Box 1, (Canadian–American Studies File), University Archives, Western Washington University, Accession 83-23.

11. Letter from W. Chance to W. G. Magnuson, May 14, 1980, Records of President's Office, Box 1, (Canadian–American Studies File), University Archives, Western Washington University, Accession 83-23.

12. Memo from R. Varley to British Columbia Students Attending WWU, May 5, 1981, Canadian–American Studies files, Canada House, Western Washington University.

13. Letter from W. M. Polk to D. Alper, August 5, 1981, Canadian–American Studies Files, Canada House, Western Washington University.

14. "Bad Neighbors," Editorial in *Vancouver Sun* (May 5, 1981) B1.

15. Letter from R. M. Bond to D. Alper, June 26, 1981, Canadian–American Studies Files. Canada House, Western Washington University.

16. Letter from P. Olscamp to H. Groh, December 22, 1981, Records of President's Office, Box 6, University Archives, Western Washington University, Accession No. 85-25.

17. Note from M. Robinson to File titled, "Proposal for Canada House-circa 1982," Special Collections, Wilson Library, Western Washington University.

18. "Proposal for Canada House-circa 1982," Special Collections, Wilson Library, Western Washington University.

19. Ibid.

20. "Students, Officials Question Faculty Club Cost," *Bellingham Herald* (June 4, 1982) 1-B.

21. Ibid.

22. Letter from J. Hitchman to S. Kelly and other university officials, January 5, 1988, Canadian–American Studies Files, Canada House, Western Washington University.

23. Ibid.

Chapter 6: National Recognition

1. Memo from J. Hitchman to Canadian Studies Faculty, February 8, 1988, Canadian–American Studies Files, Canada House, Western Washington University.

2. Consortium Planning Seminar Summary Report, September 27, 1984. Canadian–American Studies Files, Canada House, Western Washington University.

3. Quoted in "USC Pacific Coast Canadian Studies Center grant proposal (85-87)," Canadian–American Studies Files, Canada House, Western Washington University.

4. Quoted in "Distinguished Professorship of Canadian Business and Economic Relations (N.D.)," Canadian–American Studies Files, Canada House, Western Washington University.

5. Found in 1987 Ross DP Correspondence file, in Canadian–American Studies Files, Canada House, Western Washington University.

Chapter 7: The Culture Turn

1. From Report by E. Fry, "External Review of the Pacific Northwest Consortium on Canadian Studies," May 19, 1989, Canadian–American Studies Files, Canada House, Western Washington University.

2. Memorandum from R. Monahan, "The Distinguished Professorship of Canadian Culture," January 24, 1991, Canadian–American Studies Files, Canada House, Western Washington University.

3. Letter from D. Seaborn to R. Monahan, October 16, 1996, Canadian–American Studies Files, Canada House, Western Washington University.

4. Email from G. Geddes to M. Hitchcock, September 3, 1999, Canadian–American Studies Files, Canada House, Western Washington University.

5. Report from A. Smith, titled, "External Review of the Pacific Northwest Canadian Studies Center," June 14, 1996, Canadian–American Studies Files, Canada House, Western Washington University.

6. Letter from L. DeLorme to R. Monahan, May 28, 1992, Records of Provost's Office, Box 3, (International Programs/Canadian–American Studies File), University Archives, Western Washington University, Accession No. 95-94.

7. Report from D. Alper to S. Sulkin, "Long Range Plan-Canadian Studies,"

April 15, 1993, Records of President's Office, Box 13, University Archives, Western Washington University, Accession No. 95-42.

8. James Loucky, faculty member in the anthropology department, had recently been appointed Interim Director of the Center for International Studies. Loucky was a specialist on Latin America and had taught and conducted research on the U.S.-Mexico border. He had worked with several government agencies and the Fulbright Foundation and believed that hemispheric (U.S., Canada, Mexico) studies was the wave of the future and Western could leverage its strength in Canadian Studies and environmental education to be competitive in this area. Memorandum from J. Loucky to L. DeLorme, August 18, 1994, Canadian–American Studies Files, Canada House, Western Washington University.

9. Copy of article titled "Learning About Teaching Canada," August 5, 2002, Records of Provost's Office, Box 7, (Canadian–American Studies File), University Archives, Western Washington University, Accession No. 2005-27.

Chapter 8: New Border Institute

1. Quoted in, Thompson, J. H. "Playing by the New Washington Rules: The U.S.-Canada Relationship, 1994-2003," *The American Review of Canadian Studies*, 33:1 (March, 2003) 10.

2. Email correspondence from D. Little to D. Alper, April 30, 2019, Canadian–American Studies Files, Canada House, Western Washington University.

3. "Proposal for Establishing the Transportation Research Institute, 2004," Canadian–American Studies Files, Canada House, Western Washington University.

4. Press Release from Senator Murray, September 9, 2004, Canadian–American Studies Files, Canada House, Western Washington University.

5. Letter from K. Morse to P. Murray, March 5, 2005, Canadian–American Studies Files, Canada House, Western Washington University.

6. Email from A. Bodman to D. Alper, March 1, 2005, Records of Provost's Office, Box 1, (Canadian–American Studies Files), University Archives, Western Washington University, Accession No. 2009-141.

7. Email from C. Wood to D. Davidson and D. Alper, February 6, 2007, Canadian–American Studies Files, Canada House, Western Washington University.

Chapter 9: A House Matters

1. Letter from A. Bodman to ARCS Editor Search Committee, August 25, 2006, Canadian–American Studies Files, Canada House, Western

Chapter Notes

Washington University.

2. "Can-Am/BPRI Task Force Recommendation," 2012, p. 35, Canadian–American Studies Files, Canada House, Western Washington University.

3. The BPRI was created in 2005 to conduct independent, data-driven policy research to assess and (hopefully) help improve border policy making. The Canadian–American Studies academic program was aimed at fostering broad-based knowledge on matters pertaining to Canada. Each program benefitted from the work of the other. Some administrators and faculty questioned whether or not both were needed or if they should be consolidated into one unit.

4. Letter from M. Krieger to K. Morse, November 2, 2000, Canadian–American Studies Files, Canada House, Western Washington University.

5. Letter from N. Pagh to K. Morse, October 28, 2000, Canadian–American Studies Files, Canada House, Western Washington University.

6. Email from A. Bodman to D. Alper, November 21, 2000, Canadian–American Studies Files, Canada House, Western Washington University.

7. Email from K. Morse to D. Alper, November 30, 2000, Canadian–American Studies Files, Canada House, Western Washington University.

8. Eventually, the building received necessary upgrades for wireless internet. What seemed to make the difference was holding regular classes in the downstairs reception room. Somebody in the administration decided internet capability was crucial because students were taking classes in the building.

9. Email from D. Alper to K. Morse, February 28, 2008, Box 5, Records of President's Office, (Canadian–American Studies File), University Archives, Western Washington University, Accession No. 2016-18. The William D. Ruckelshaus Center at the University of Washington was created to bring government, business, conservation groups, citizens and academics together to develop solution to complex problems facing Washington state.

10. The Culture professorship position was never given the originally promised full time FTE. Still only at half time funding, the position nonetheless enabled the Center to occasionally hire part time faculty to cover needed courses in the humanities.

Chapter 10: A Border Runs Through it

1. These comments were part of a speech, "Beyond the Border Introductory Remarks" given at The Beyond the Border Dialogue at Age One: Policy and Political Implications for the Pacific Northwest Conference, Seattle, February 10, 2012, Canadian–American Studies Files, Canada House, Western Washington University.

2. Letter from C. Gregoire on the occasion of the Center for Canadian–American Studies 40th Anniversary, April 28, 2011, Canadian–American Studies Files, Canada House, Western Washington University.

3. Donnelly, R. "Unruly Children of a Common Mother: Canada–US Center at WWU Celebrates 40 years of Dynamic Relationship," *Cascadia Weekly* (May 4, 2011) 11.

4. Jameson, Elizabeth, "Both Sides Now: 'Parallel' lines Across Binational Pasts," *American Review of Canadian Studies* 42:4 (2012) 489-496.

5. Memorandum from C. Riordan titled, "Request for Participation in Canadian–American Studies/Border Policy Institute Task Force," August 27, 2012, Records from Provost's Files, Box 4, (Canadian–American Studies File), University Archives, Western Washington University, Accession No. 2017-12.

6. Ibid.

7. "Canadian–American Studies/Border Policy Research Institute Task Force Recommendation, December 2012." Canadian–American Studies Files, Canada House, Western Washington University, p. 2.

8. Ibid, p. 25.

9. Ibid.

10. Ibid., p. 1.

11. Ibid., p. 9

12. Ibid., p. 2

13. Ibid., p. 5.

14. Ibid., p. 1.

15. "Western Appoints First Salish Sea Director," *Western Front Online* (July 8, 2017), https://www.westernfrontonline.com/2017/07/08/western-appoints-first-salish-sea-institute-director/

Acknowledgments

My sincerest thanks go to Catherine Wallace for the many ways she contributed to this book. A professional journalist and editor, Cat contributed more hours than I can count overseeing all aspects of the process—from reading and copyediting chapter drafts to selecting and formatting the archive photos used in this book. As managing editor of the *American Review of Canadian Studies* for over nine years, Cat encouraged me to undertake the project in the first place, giving up many summer afternoons to help sort scores of dusty and water-damaged file boxes in the basement of Canada House with me. She expertly guided the organization of the project from beginning to end, gently steering me away from too much "academic-speak"—always a danger for a university professor by trade.

Several archivists and librarians at Western Washington University went out of their way to help me in any way they could. In particular, my deep appreciation to University Archivist Tony Kurtz, for his guidance and assistance in digging through archival boxes that spanned several collections.

An enormous debt of gratitude is owed to Special Collections Manager, Tamara Belts, for locating key documents and also for her decades-long work in keeping Western Washington University history alive. Also, thanks to Elizabeth Joffrion, Director of Heritage Resources, and Ruth Steele, Center for Pacific Northwest Studies Archivist.

Many thanks to Rachel Johnson at Village Books in Bellingham for facilitating the printing and marketing of this book, and to Marla Tyree for her clever design work on its attractive cover.

Two scholars and friends I want to thank particularly: Milton Krieger's enthusiasm for the project was more important in motivating me than he knows, and Barry Gough's recollections about his early years at Western were incredibly valuable. His passion for Canadian Studies continues to inspire.

But most of all, my deepest appreciation is saved for my wife, Jan, who believed this story was worth telling and cheered me on every step of the way.

About the Author

Donald K. Alper, Emeritus Professor of Political Science at Western Washington University, is the former director of Western's Center for Canadian–American Studies (1993–2014) and founder and director of the Border Policy Research Institute (2005–2014). He is renowned for his advancement of Canadian Studies in the United States and is credited with building bridges between the two nations through his personal, professional, and academic achievements in outreach, research, publication, and service. He holds a Ph.D. in political science from the University of British Columbia. For more than forty years, he taught courses on Canadian politics and Canada–United States political relations. He has authored numerous articles and book chapters and co-authored two books dealing with environmental, security and other aspects of the Canada–United States borderlands. He was elected president of the Association for Canadian Studies in the United States and won the prestigious Donner Medal for excellence in Canadian Studies in the U.S. in 2007. He is retired and lives in Bellingham, Washington, with his wife Jan.

www.ingramcontent.com/pod-product-compliance
Lightning Source LLC
Chambersburg PA
CBHW031245290426
44109CB00012B/435